CIW 1995 p 224 one-cent campaign
2005!

'non-automated Farming jobs:
p18) Mushroom picker    + tomatoes?
de-tasseling corn       Citrus?
apple picking

# Out of the Sea and Into The Fire

## Immigration from Latin America to the U.S. in the Global Age

### Kari Lydersen

*no*

Common Courage Press        Monroe, Maine

ISBN 1-56751-302-6 paper
ISBN 1-56751-303-4 cloth

**Library of Congress Cataloging-in-Publication Data is available on request from the publisher**

Common Courage Press
121 Red Barn Road
Monroe, ME 04951
800-497-3207

FAX (207) 525-3068
orders-info@commoncouragepress.com

See our website for e versions of this book.
www.commoncouragepress.com

Printed in Canada
**First Printing**

Dedication: To my parents Pat and Ken, who write about everything from molecular biology to monsters who can't be scary.

# Acknowledgements

Most of all I want to thank all the people who shared their stories with me, and often their homes and meals as well. I feel like it is an honor and a privilege to have spoken with so many people and experienced their courage, generosity and determination first hand. Also I want to thank all the tireless community organizers, advocates and activists who took time out of their 24-hour-a-day work schedules to talk with me and help me coordinate visits and interviews. These names are far too many to mention here, but most of them are quoted and mentioned in the book. To all of them, and anyone whom I inadvertently forgot to mention, a million thanks.

Here I just want to mention some of the people who are not otherwise named in the book, and who provided invaluable assistance, editing or encouragement. They are:

Jason Wallach; Allan Gomez; Victoria Cervantes; Maribel Ortega; Miguel Vazquez; Benjamin Prado (Raza Rights Coalition); Sister Susan Mika; Brian Payne, Greg Asbed and Laura Geromino with the Coalition of Immokalee Workers; John K. Wilson; Scott Sherman; Sasha Abramsky; Robert Pierre; Brian Awehali; Joel Schalit; Daniel Burton Rose; Billy Upski Wimsatt; Rhoda Rae Gutierrez; Eve Tulbert; Tricia Hackett; and Faith Attaguile.

Also thanks to the different media outlets which published variations of some of these chapters or other stories on these topics along the way: Conscious Choice, LiP Magazine, Punk Planet, Impact Press, Alternet, Clamor Magazine, Hasta Cuando, Third Coast Press, Americas Connection and IndyMedia.

And of course thanks to Greg Bates and Common Courage Press for publishing this book and all the inspiring and educational books they publish.

# Contents

Acknowledgements      iv

Notes      1

Introduction: Life on the Margins      3

## Part I
## Latin America

1. Another Piece in the Puzzle:      23
   Oaxacan Fishermen and Farmers
   Anticipate Plan Puebla-Panama

2. Who is Destroying the Jungle?      37
   Politics and Preservation in Montes Azules, Chiapas

3. Ecuador and the Almighty Dollar      51

4. From the Mountains to the Sea:      61
   The Fight for Land in Honduras

5. "Killer Coke:" Global Refresher or Represser?      71

6. Teatro Trono: Bolivians Act Out      83

## Part II
## The Border

7. Trashing the Border, Taking Human Lives:      119
   The Residue of Free Trade and Industry in Tijuana

8. Las Desaparecidas:      129
   The Lost Women of Ciudad Juarez

9. Poisonous Profits:      143
   The Malignant Underside of Reynosa's Maquila Zone

10. Casualties of War:      155
    The Border 's Death Zone

## Part III
## The United States

11. Picking Mushrooms and Killing Cows:      182
    Immigration in Small Town Illinois

12. In the Shadows of "America's Finest City:"     191
    The Ripple Effects of Sept. 11 in San Diego

13. Not in My Backyard:     203
    The Albany Park Workers Center

14. Pulling Injustice Up From the Roots:     217
    The Coalition of Immokalee Workers

15. Longing for Home; Hoping to Stay:     231
    An Immigrant's Life in Nebraska

## Part IV
### Profiles

16. Jose Oliva: Coming Full Circle     243

17. Alexy Lanza: "Wherever I see injustice…"     249

18. Neris Gonzalez: The Seeds of Change     257

Conclusion     265

Glossary of Terms and Acronyms     267

Notes     271

About the Author     277

# Notes

The title *Out of the Sea and Into the Fire* refers to a composite image of immigrants who are forced to leave their homelands and ancestral ways of life to make the arduous trip across the border and search for work in the U.S.—for example a Oaxacan fisherman who can no longer earn a living from the sea, who risks his life to cross blazing deserts and freezing mountains into the U.S., where he joins the thousands of Latin American immigrants working in slaughterhouses, tomato fields, kitchens or doing the other work U.S. citizens are rarely willing to do.

Unless otherwise indicated, all of these stories come from personal interviews I conducted between 2000 and 2004 and scenes I witnessed during trips to Latin America, the border and different parts of the U.S. Most of the quotes are translated from Spanish, either by myself or others.

In some cases conditions described by the subjects of the stories could not be otherwise verified; in the text these anecdotes are attributed to the subjects. Even if these situations did not happen or exist exactly as the subjects described them, it can be fairly assumed that the overall implications and effects that they describe are indicative of the realities that many people experience.

Detail of "Cataclysm," a mural by Marcos Raya.

# INTRODUCTION
## Life on the Margins

Eduardo Galeano's epic history of the region is called "The Open Veins of Latin America."

Journalist Alma Guillermoprieto's collection of dispatches from Latin America is titled "The Heart That Bleeds," in reference to a lyric from a postmodern ranchera singer.[1]

In "The Jaguar Smile," his memoir of a trip to post-revolution Nicaragua, novelist Salman Rushdie describes the raggedy determination and desperation of the tiny rain-soaked country, where everyone is a poet.

From the works of famous writers like Gabriel Garcia Marquez and Pablo Neruda to the words of everyday peasants and laborers, Latin America is often described in sensual and macabre terms relating to pain, blood and sorrow as well as overwhelming passion and beauty. The bottom line of it all is suffering, seemingly endless and exquisite suffering.

Like a beautiful woman who is doomed to abuse and tragedy by her beauty, the region lends itself well to this perception. Everybody wants a piece of her, and her body is torn and tortured in the process.

The region is so lush in natural beauty and resources—gold, oil, bio-diversity, to name just a few—yet so tortured by exploitation, war, disease, hunger. It has been ravaged by succeeding waves of conquest over the centuries, from the war-like Aztecs and Incas to the gold-hungry Spaniards to the current wave of U.S. speculators looking for cheap beachfront property. Over the past century Latin American countries have been squeezed from the outside by colonialism and foreign investment and intervention while being bled from the inside by notoriously corrupt politicians and leaders. Brothers have killed brothers in countless civil wars, and husbands and daughters have disappeared in the night, their bodies later found mutilated, in the various "dirty wars."

Even earthquakes, hurricanes and other natural disasters seem to hit Latin America with special vengeance, as if the havoc wrought on it by humankind weren't bad enough.

Many have come to see this ever-present sense of tragedy, including violence, death, sickness and poverty, as simply part of life, embodied in the timeless image of La Llorona, the beautiful, proud and tortured woman who is forever weeping.

But the latest forces to wreak havoc on the region can not be dismissed as part of some ancient curse, some resigned acceptance of the fact that to live is to suffer.

The biggest destroyer of lives in Latin America today is in fact far removed from the spiritual and magical realm.

It is something planned out behind closed doors in boardrooms continents away, by men in suits who will never visit the home of a peasant in the mountains of Ecuador or a fisherman on the coast of Mexico. The forces of economic globalization, manifested through corporate deals and free trade agreements, have transformed life for the people of Latin America more dramatically than the conquistadors.

Since the North American Free Trade Agreement (NAFTA) took effect on New Year's Day in 1994, numerous statistics and studies show that poverty has increased sharply in Mexico and malnutrition, infant death and its other attendant symptoms have worsened.

"Income distribution has worsened during the NAFTA years," says a November 2003 report from the Interhemispheric Research Center (IRC). "The number of households living in poverty has grown 80 percent since 1984 and NAFTA did not redress this trend. Today, 70 percent of Mexico's population lives below the poverty line. Rural poverty is rampant and migration has increased. The toll in terms of health and malnutrition is dramatic, with 60 percent of indigenous children suffering severe malnutrition."[2]

A study by the Carnegie Endowment for International

Peace found that as it neared its 10<sup>th</sup> anniversary, NAFTA had failed to generate substantial job growth in Mexico and had hurt thousands of subsistence farmers there, while having only a miniscule positive effect on jobs in the U.S. Real wages were lower, unemployment higher and economic inequality greater in Mexico after a decade of NAFTA despite higher productivity.

"Between 1994 and 2003...only three million jobs were created in the formal sector," the IRC reports. "Thus, 60 percent of the demand for new jobs remains unsatisfied, forcing people to explore other survival strategies in the so-called informal sector."[3]

This should not be surprising even to someone unschooled in economics. Since the virtual obliteration of tariffs has allowed U.S. companies to flood Mexico with subsidized corn and other commodities which it can produce more cheaply than Mexicans can, the local markets for these goods have been decimated. Mexican farmers who were making a subsistence level income before suddenly have nowhere to sell their goods.

In 10 years an estimated five million Mexican farmers have been put out of business by NAFTA.[4] Many have fled their hometowns and lives as peasants to look for work in the cities, and failing that, to head for the promised land north of the border. Contrary to popular opinion most immigrants aren't starry-eyed over making it to the land of Nikes and "Baywatch;" most don't want to leave their homeland, but they have no choice.

Some have no choice because they cannot even feed themselves or their families; others might be able to eke out a living but they know that in Mexico they will never be able to do the things that ideally should be every human being's right— to study, to travel, to dream.

"I knew if I kept working in the fields in this small town [in Zacatecas, Mexico] I'd never get out of the cycle of poverty, I could work my whole life without ever being able to give something to my family," said Gerardo Reyes, a 26-year-old immigrant farm worker and community organizer with the Coalition of Immokalee Workers in South Florida. "I wanted to create something, to have something to offer. So I came here."

Since NAFTA started forcing scores of Mexicans to head for the border, the zone of maquilas (multinational factories) hugging the border conveniently expanded to take advantage of their labor. Though maquilas existed before NAFTA, they were made much more profitable by the free trade provisions.

While NAFTA covers only Mexico (and Canada to the north, of course), its effects have been felt as well throughout Central and even South America. Whatever Mexico suffers, Guatemala and its other neighbors to the south suffer perhaps even more intensely, having been more destitute to begin with. As the U.S. beefs up its border with Mexico, so Mexico increases its border security with Guatemala. As more Mexicans are forced off their land and scrabble to earn a living in the cities, so life is tougher too for Central American migrants in Mexico—you could call it trans-continental trickle-down border security and trickle-down poverty.

And now a raft of new free trade agreements are on the table, chief among them the U.S.-Central America Free Trade Agreement (CAFTA) and the Free Trade Area of the Americas (FTAA), often called "NAFTA on steroids,"[5] which would expand NAFTA-like provisions to 34 countries,[6] promising a $13 trillion market with 800 million potential consumers[7] but likely providing increasing poverty.

In addition to these specific free trade agreements, for at least the past two decades the developing world has also been harmed by various government and corporate policies meant to maximize global profits and keep countries running in a way that is conducive to free trade. Structural adjustment, austerity and privatization programs mandated by the World Bank and International Monetary Fund have torn at the social and economic fabric of life in Bolivia, Peru, Ecuador and other impoverished Latin American countries.

And regulations set by the World Trade Organization (WTO) which supersede countries' own constitutions often take away the few avenues of recourse that might have been available to exploited third world workers and gut almost all environmental protections in these ecologically raped countries.

In "The Heart That Bleeds," Guillermoprieto writes of the institution of free trade and domestic austerity measures in Bolivia in the 1980s that resulted in skyrocketing unemployment and hunger. She notes that these effects were fully expected by the architects of the program. The "programmed misery" experienced by masses of the country's poor "was predicted and taken into account by the planners," who went ahead with their plans nonetheless.[8]

Latin America isn't the only region being pummeled by free trade—globalization is causing increasing poverty and misery in so-called "developing" and "third world" countries around the globe. In fact Mexico is already becoming a bit passe as a cash cow in the global economy, with maquilas increasingly going to China where labor costs only one fourth what it does in Mexico. The Mexican government has reported that 500 of Mexico's formerly 3,700 maquilas shut down between 2001 and late 2003, at a cost of 218,000 jobs.

Meanwhile, the juxtaposition of neighboring "first world" and "third world" countries bound together in an unbalanced free trade relationship has created similar border and immigration problems throughout the world. For example the border dynamics between Morocco and Spain have many parallels to the U.S.- Mexican border. Young Moroccan women looking for a better life pay smugglers to take them across the border and then end up working as prostitutes in border regions in Spain, just like Mexicans do in the U.S. And just as hundreds of immigrants die every year trying to cross the desert into the U.S., in October 2003 over 50 African immigrants died in rickety boats at sea as they tried to reach islands off the coast of Italy.[9]

Scholar/journalist Mike Davis notes that, "The human toll from the new world (b)order grows inexorably. According to human rights groups, nearly 4,000 immigrants and refugees have died at the gates of Europe since 1993: drowned at sea, blown up in minefields, or suffocated in freight containers. Hundreds, perhaps thousands more, have perished in desperate attempts to cross the Sahara desert simply to reach Europe's borders."[10]

Though the suffering and strife caused by borders is not unique to the U.S.-Latin America relationship, it is fair to say that U.S. citizens have a special responsibility in regards to this dynamic. Mexican and other Latin American immigrants make up a significant portion of most small towns and major cities across the U.S. While there is no official number, it is often reported that there are over six million undocumented Mexican immigrants in the U.S. today, and hundreds of thousands more undocumented people from other parts of Latin America. Despite an increasingly militarized border that has made crossing a sometimes deadly undertaking, people continue to come as much as ever before.

It is a sad and at times seemingly hopeless situation, with the stories of farmers displaced from their land and families ripped apart; people dying on the border at the hands of vigilantes, smugglers or the elements; and immigrants encountering exploitation, racism and police brutality in the U.S.

But just as it is famous for suffering, Latin America has also always been famous for struggle. Just within the past few years the populace of Bolivia overthrew a president; indigenous and campesino activists in Mexico prevented the building of an airport which would have displaced them; and poor and working class Venezuelans took to the streets to defend their president against the interests of the U.S. and the Venezuelan upper class. And the Zapatistas in Chiapas, who launched their movement on Jan. 1, 1994 as a direct declaration of war on NAFTA, continue to creatively and doggedly fight for dignity and autonomy even after a decade of grueling low-intensity warfare.

So along with showing the poverty and pain that has been caused by globalization and free trade, I also want to show the strength and resistance of communities in Latin America and Latin American immigrants in the U.S. This strength is manifested in their fights to hold maquila owners accountable for the health effects of working with toxic chemicals; in their determination to do whatever it takes to cross the border; in their ability to work 16 hours a day in low-paying jobs in the U.S. while still finding the energy to laugh and joke; in their passionate fights for immigrants' rights even as they risk being deported themselves for their activism.

This spirit of unwavering determination, courage and even joy was embodied as members of the Coalition of Immokalee Workers from Haiti, Guatemala, Mexico and other countries took time off from their back-breaking work to march 34 miles from Ft. Lauderdale to Miami in November 2003 to protest the FTAA.[11]

Or when Latin American immigrants joined Eastern European immigrants, African-Americans and others to take to the streets of major cities and demand better pay and labor rights during the Justice for Janitors campaign.[12]

Or when hundreds of immigrants from all over the world piled on buses to converge in Washington D.C. for the Immigrant Workers Freedom Rides of 2003.[13]

Three profiles finish this book, a selection from among countless examples of what Latin American immigration is all about. These are the images that dwarf even the most formidable and depressing stories of poverty, repression, displacement and exploitation. These are images of pure hope.

In the words of Norman Ospina, a Colombian immigrant and community organizer in Chicago, "immigrants are victimized but are NOT victims."

"You can look at immigration as forced migration or as resistance," said Ospina. "It's a matter of, 'I can't make it here, so I'm going to cross the border and make a better life.' They're risking their life to cross the border and working hard every single day. You can't call that anything but resistance. We're dealing with people who know how to resist, who know how to fight."

*Part I*

# LATIN AMERICA

An indigenous woman walks by graffiti in San Cristobal, Chiapas, declaring that under capitalism, peace and war are the same thing. Photo by Kari Lydersen.

The land of the Garifuna on the coast of Honduras can best be described as paradise, sparkling blue water and white sand dotted by palm trees and drenched every evening in beautiful sunsets. The Garifuna are fighting to hold on to this slice of heaven in the face of developers who want to build five star hotels.

The land claimed by indigenous Tulopane campesinos from Montaña de la Flor in the mountains of Honduras is also beautiful, small plots of corn growing among majestic pines with fingers of mist swirling through.

They are fighting over this land with a neighboring band of campesinos who they call Los Invincibles, or The Invincibles.

The land of the indigenous Chol people in Montes Azules, part of the Lacondon Jungle in Chiapas, Mexico, is characterized by sudden and violent rainstorms, palms and mahogany trees laden with hanging vines, and a wide greenish brown river that stretches through it all, inhabited by 15-foot-long vicious yellow crocodiles. Here, small communities of indigenous people are also engaged in a daily struggle to hold on to their land, facing off against another indigenous group who are aligned with the government and run tourist outfits in the jungle.

While these conflicts might seem local and even petty on the surface, on a deeper level they are examples of how the forces of globalization—of trade, tourism, resource exploitation—are affecting daily life in communities across Latin America, and ultimately forcing many people to migrate from their homeland and often all the way to the U.S.

For centuries, struggles over land have been a defining component of life in Latin America. Land is not only a way to feed and house one's family, it also has almost cosmic emotional, spiritual and intellectual significance.

The notion of land ownership in Latin America is notably different than in the modern U.S. Many indigenous cultures historically didn't believe in or even have a concept of land ownership, seeing themselves in a symbiotic and mutually nurturing relationship with the earth.

As various parties have staked out claims over the decades, different and often fluid ways of defining what land ownership means and how it is established have developed. As farming or cattle-raising have become the primary means of sustenance throughout much of the region, even indigenous groups that would have eschewed land ownership in the past have been forced to participate in the ritual.

Land has always been unequally distributed throughout Latin America, as in most of the world. The Latifundios or haciendas where a wealthy rancher lorded over peasants in a semi-feudal system is a classic part of Latin American history.

Unlike in the U.S., however, there is also a strong tradition of agrarian reform throughout the region, and taking land from the rich to redistribute to the poor and landless is an accepted philosophy and often part of national policy. The land reform laws on the books in Honduras, Mexico and other countries are actually truly radical by U.S. standards, but of course they are far different in practice than on paper. In most countries record-keeping throughout the years has been chaotic at best, and two or more parties often have titles to the same piece of land. Different government agencies also often work in opposition to each other, with one agency actually supporting peasants' right to a certain piece of land, while another government agency is trying to seize it from them.

Throughout Latin America, militant land takeovers are a key form of struggle and survival, and in many countries they are an officially recognized way of obtaining legal title to land.

These land struggles often have a Wild West air to them, with neighbors and even family members duking out their territorial disputes with fists, sticks, knives and guns. Wealthy large landowners, corporations and institutions often hire thugs or police officers acting essentially as thugs to terrorize peasants involved in land occupations.

While these day-to-day skirmishes over land may seem

petty or purely local, the larger issue underlying them is the age-old struggle between the haves and have-nots. In this day and age, this struggle is manifested in the conflict between regular, poor people trying to make a living and multinational corporations trying to maximize their profits, seizing land for hotels, oil drilling, bio-prospecting or logging.

When Antonio Mejía Vazquez was killed by a neighboring family known as Los Aguilares in the tiny K'an Akil hamlet in Chiapas in August 2002, for example, it appeared on the surface to be a family feud having to do with water rights and a small piece of land.

But in the larger sense the crime can clearly be seen as part of the global conflict, since K'An Akil is an autonomous Zapatista-aligned community and the Aguilares include former military members armed by the government. In situations like this across the region, the government or corporate forces capitalize on local feuds and micro-conflicts to carry out their dirty work, arming and giving impunity to the people whose actions serve their aims, and withholding protection and justice from those, like Mejía, who exist in opposition.

There are countless communities exhibiting remarkable tenacity and courage by carrying out land occupations, ranging from the famous Movimiento Sin Tierra (Landless Workers Movement) of peasants in Brazil all the way up to countless urban squatter communities of maquila workers near the U.S.-Mexico border. And often these land struggles are effective, with the people gaining either legal rights to their land or living on and working the land without legal title in the face of constant threats. But peasants and indigenous people are constantly forced off their land, either physically displaced or forced economically to look for work elsewhere.

While the struggles over land and between the rich and the poor are age-old paradigms, globalization has added a new dimension. Now, many of the powerful parties trying to seize land are not just local heavyweights but multinational companies.

Graffiti in Tegucigalpa, Honduras decries the free trade agreement ALCA (The Spanish acronym for the FTAA). Photo by Kari Lydersen.

And in countless cases the peasant's nemesis in these land struggles is not a physical entity but an abstract economic concept—the fact that with the obliteration of tariffs and the imposition of other free trade measures, they can no longer make a living on their land.

When people are displaced from their land, globalization has altered the economy and social structures throughout the region so much that rather than being able to find work in a nearby city or town, many people will head all the way to the U.S.

"In Latin America traditionally economic hardships meant people migrated from rural areas to urban areas," said Jose Oliva, a Guatemalan native who immigrated to the U.S. with his family as a child. "When work was unobtainable in urban areas, they'd migrate to the U.S. People aren't coming because of American prosperity and the American dream. They're coming because American corn is cheaper in Mexico than Mexican corn, so they can't do subsistence farming like they did before."

This exodus from Latin America to the U.S. has had a massive ripple effect on life in Latin America. With increased U.S. border security, it is hard for men to even come back to visit their families, and many of them start second families in the U.S.

"There are whole communities without men," said Victor Muñoz, a Chihuahua, Mexico native who works as a labor organizer in El Paso. "They've all gone to the U.S. Before they could cross back and forth easily so they could return every few months, but that's not the case now that the border is tighter."

Along with cheap corn and the like, globalization has produced a more sinister export which has inspired terror in Latin American cities. Gangs like Mara 18 and Mara Salvatrucha have developed in L.A. and other U.S. cities. Members of these gangs who are deported to their home countries are responsible for a huge increase in violent crime, including beheadings and mutilations in places like San Salvador, Tegucigalpa and Guatemala City over the past few years.

The back and forth of immigrants has also had a huge effect on Latin American culture. U.S. hip hop music, surfer/skateboarder fashion and Spanglish slang have spread throughout the hemisphere. There seem to be more American flag decals and T-shirts in evidence in the working class city of Guayaquil, Ecuador, for example, than in any U.S. city, even though people in Guayaquil are also quick to talk about how their lives have gotten harder since the country switched to the dollar as the official currency.

Many Latin Americans have a complicated love-hate relationship with the U.S. There is obviously a huge fascination with U.S. culture and people are proud of their family members who have forged lives in the U.S. But there is also widespread awareness of and resentment toward the U.S. for its foreign policy and economic influence. Though multinational corporations, the World Bank, the International Monetary Fund and the World Trade Organization are all global institutions, rightly or wrongly people see the U.S. as the driving force behind them all. The streets of any major city in Latin America are scrawled with graffiti decrying the U.S., President Bush and the war in Iraq along with the IMF, FTAA and privatization plans. In the coastal city of Coro in Venezuela, resentment toward the U.S. is so strong that there is a large sign pledging solidarity with deposed Iraqi president Saddam Hussein on one of the major streets.

South American women visiting Chicago for a conference on "Women Taking Land" in the spring of 2003 lashed out against the effects globalization is having on their countries and the U.S. role in perpetuating free trade on the backs of the poor.

"Globalization has closed the spaces to recuperate land," said Rosemeri Witcel, 30, a member of the Movimiento Sin Tierra (Landless Workers Movement), the radical peasants group in Brazil. "We have to fight against the landowners who want huge areas of land. Brazil imports so much food from the U.S., but we don't want this. We're capable of producing our own food without dependency on an imperialist nation that wants to dominate us."

In Mexico and Central America, people fear massive displacement from the Plan Puebla Panama (PPP), a plan for a huge "dry canal" composed of high speed railroads and highways lined with eucalyptus plantations, industrial shrimp farms, maquilas and other industries. On the lovely coast of Oaxaca, one of the key areas included in the PPP, small fishermen and goat herders are seeing their way of life slip away as major industry takes hold.

Colombian native Luis Adolfo Cardona was also forced to leave his homeland as a direct result of the way global business is carried out. He won political asylum in the U.S. because paramilitary members were trying to murder him to punish him for his unionizing activities at a bottling plant for Coca-Cola—a beverage which epitomizes the borderless world of global consumerism.

It might seem impossible for poor, often illiterate peasants and indigenous people to fight the plans of institutions like the IMF and the World Bank, which will lead to their impoverishment and displacement through measures like privatizing their water—making them pay for a resource that had long been free as the air they breath. Or by making it harder for them to sell their corn,  since subsidized U.S. imports will be cheaper than crops grown locally. Or by seizing their land for multinational companies to drill oil or build tourist resorts, with the justification that it will help the national economy as a whole.

But there is a long tradition of popular education in Latin America, and people do see knowledge about free trade and its effects as one of their most important tools or weapons.

Raising awareness of globalization and its effects both in Latin America and in the U.S. is one of the main goals of Teatro Trono, a youth street theater group formed by kids from juvenile detention centers and the streets of the impoverished highlands of El Alto and La Paz, Bolivia in 1989. Youth from the troupe have traveled around the U.S. and Europe performing and spreading their message.

"We're working to help people understand that local problems have international significance," said Teatro Trono founder Ivan Nogales. "The defense of our gas, the defense of our natural resources. International organizations (like the IMF and World Bank) defend the interests of transnational companies. In Bolivia it is very clear. The question is, how do we change this? The U.S. has such immense power, it's not easy."

Nogales and the teenagers who traveled with him to Chicago in the fall of 2003 were thrilled to hear news of the popular uprising that overthrew Bolivian president "Goni" Sánchez de Lozada. Bolivians were furious at Lozada for trying to push through IMF-mandated privatization and austerity programs and to sell the country's natural gas to the U.S.

"Bolivia is one of the calls to attention among many—Ecuador, Argentina, Venezuela," said Nogales. "Bolivia is a beautiful example because it shows we aren't content, we are tired of so many abuses. [IMF-mandated programs and other global economic policies] don't solve anything. Each time there is more poverty, more kids on the street, more malnutrition. The crisis is getting worse and worse. The world needs to see what's happening because of these policies."

Fisherman in this idyllic town on the coast of Oaxaca, Mexico are finding it harder and harder to make a liviing. Photo by Kari Lydersen.

# CHAPTER ONE

# Another Piece in the Puzzle

## Oaxacan Fishermen and Farmers Anticipate Plan Puebla-Panama

The inhabitants of San Antonio Tuxtla haven't heard much about globalization.

In their small town, made up of thatch and mud huts, two basketball courts and a smattering of rectangular concrete structures nestled in the tropical mountains of the Isthmus of Tehuantepec in Oaxaca, Mexico, life goes on much as it has for decades, even centuries. The residents of San Antonio, indigenous Mixe Indians, make their living off farming corn and other crops in the wet, hilly area. Chickens and turkeys meander freely between homes and young children ride bareback on horses along the dirt road through town. Most of the residents are Catholic, but they still practice original Mixe traditions.

Though terms like "World Bank," "NAFTA" and most recently "Plan Puebla-Panama" are only mysterious, abstract terms to them, they are fully aware of the concrete effect globalization and free trade has had on their lives. They note that corn and coffee prices are steadily dropping, and it is harder and harder for them to make sales because Mexicans can buy corn imported from Iowa more cheaply than corn grown right around the corner. The government assistance program for farmers known as Procampo has not been a big help to them, members of the Council of Elders in the community told a group of visitors in August 2001, because men are required to pick up their checks in the city, spending a full workday and no small amount of money on transportation to the railroad town of Matias Romero about a two hour drive over dirt roads. Once in town, one of the elders noted, the men are tempted to spend their checks in bars.

The residents of Playa Cangrejo, an idyllic fishing village and local vacation spot on the Pacific coast not far from San Antonio, also have seen life changing because of globalization. Isaias "Chayon" Seferino Martinez used to make his living as a fisherman, going out every morning and evening in a small boat with an outboard motor to catch fish in nets.

"He loves the sea," said his wife, Julia Fuentes Avendaño, who runs Palapa El Chayon, one of a string of thatched roof restaurants that line the beach, serving residents of the area and nearby cities who come to eat fresh seafood and sleep in hammocks on the beautiful beach for short vacations. "He misses it."

Fishing and the restaurant stopped bringing in enough money, and now Martinez gets up at 5 a.m. every morning for a long taxi and bus ride to Juchitan, where he works in an electronics store. He often stays overnight in Juchitan for days at a time while he's working there, or if he returns home it is not until 10 p.m., only to leave at 5 a.m. again.

Meanwhile Avendaño serves fish, shrimp, Coronas and Fresca sodas to the smattering of local tourists who come through, shooing away flies and a playful puppy named Whiskey as she works. Occasionally live crabs will sidle right through the sandy restaurant area, providing endless entertainment for Whiskey. Every morning before dawn the crew of young boys who still fish the area push their small motorboats through the sand into the water, and occasionally a youth will drive a herd of goats by along the beach.

The setting appears idyllic, but times are tough.

The area was devastated by Hurricane Paulina in 1997, Avendaño said, and the government did nothing to help them rebuild. Many people are kept away by the storm-damaged, difficult dirt road that stretches several miles to the beach from the main paved road. Tourists have also been diverted to the better-known beaches of Huatulco further west, an area formerly populated by indigenous locals who were moved off their land to make way for a Cancun-like resort area. Local tourism has picked up recently at Playa Cangrejo, said Avendaño on a steamy, mosquito-filled day in August 2001, but it is harder to feed the tourists because the fish have been getting smaller and smaller off the beach, possibly because of weather changes and also because of contamination from the Pemex oil refinery, one of the country's largest refineries, in the port city of Salina Cruz about 20 miles away.

Martinez feels like the Salina Cruz Pemex refinery has already had a devastating effect on local life.

"When they built the refinery, they said it would create jobs. But it has created unemployment. You can't do agriculture in the area anymore because Pemex is diverting 90 percent of the (fresh) water. You can't fish because it is polluting the water. There used to be about 100 fishermen in our area, now there are only 30. They are leaving for jobs in the north and in the U.S."

"This is an example of public spaces fighting to survive against privatization," said Carlos Beas Torres, a leader of the indigenous rights group UCIZONI, as he sat on the beach at dusk, swatting mosquitoes away and gazing out at the sea. Beas has one foot in the academic world, where he is an anthropologist who has traveled the world giving talks, and one foot in the world of grassroots indigenous organizing, the realm where he spends most of his time. Playa Cangrejo is a favorite get-away of his, as well as a perfect example of the social and economic pressures bearing down on the local people.

"They are being squeezed between Pemex on one side and the tourist industry [in Huatulco] on the other side," he said.

Oily black residue can be found coating the sand of Playa Cangrejo, and local environmentalists and fishermen say the refinery has had a definite negative effect on the coast line and the marine life in the area.

In August 2002 a group of 80 fishermen blockaded the oil refinery in Salina Cruz demanding compensation for damages they claim were caused by a diesel fuel leak that occurred when a pipeline was illegally tapped four months earlier.[14]

Despite the fact that Oaxaca produces a huge proportion of the country's oil, gasoline prices are high in the area, equivalent to prices in the U.S.

Pemex, Mexico's nationalized oil industry, was once heavily subsidized. But in the '80s the government began to change its policy to make Pemex more profitable. Thousands of union workers were laid off, and concessions for services, exploration and even drilling were awarded to foreign companies in ways that skirted the constitutional prohibitions against privatizing the industry. President Vicente Fox backed off on his plans to fully privatize Pemex after massive national outcry, but since then he has expanded oil-related service contracts for foreign companies. The country has also been under major pressure from the U.S. to open the industry up to private foreign investment.

If the industry is privatized, the refinery at Salina Cruz will likely increase its capacity and be further deregulated, increasing the strain on the environment and the local population.

"The privatization of Pemex, partially administrated, but secretly and systematically promoted by the federal government, doesn't only imply that the principal source of wealth and national sovereignty will be pawned off to foreigners, it also implies that Mexicans that live above these oil reserves will be violently removed," wrote analyst Andres Barreda in the daily La Jornada in 1999.[15]

The increasing economic squeeze on indigenous and native people like the residents of Playa Cangrejo and San Antonio has been an ongoing story over the last few decades of Mexico's history, as globalization and free trade have moved forward at a steady pace.

Right now, however, the delicate rain forests and coastal regions and the indigenous populations are at a critical juncture, hanging on the precipice of an unprecedented, sweeping free trade-related project that if it goes through could destroy countless ecological habitats and indigenous cultures forever. This project is the Plan Puebla-Panama (PPP), a pet cause of Mexican President Vicente Fox developed in conjunction with the U.S.-based Inter-American Development Bank (IDB). The PPP is a plan of tremendous scope, a $4.5 billion proposal that would create a so-called "dry canal" for international trade through all of Central America and southern Mexico, ranging as the name suggests from Panama all the way up to the state of Puebla in central Mexico and beyond. It would include a super-highway, railways and an electrical network, powered partly by new hydro-electric dams included in the project.[16]

The "canal" would be lined with maquilas and mass-scale, industrial shrimp and eucalyptus farms, petrochemical operations and mineral excavation, exploiting the area's rich natural resources and the potential cheap labor available throughout Mexico's small towns and indigenous communities. The canal would provide immediate transport for eucalyptus lumber—a non-indigenous weed of a tree known for wiping out whole native ecosystems—and mass-produced shrimp and maquila goods. The shrimp farms would largely be cultivating non-native species of shrimp from the Philippines and other areas, driving local shrimp fishermen out of business and infecting local shrimp populations with foreign bacteria and diseases. The canal would also be used largely for transport of goods and raw materials that neither originate nor are sold in Mexico or Central America—goods made cheaply in India and China on their way to the U.S. and Europe, for example.

While the PPP as Fox has dreamed it up encompasses all of Mexico and Central America, the Isthmus of Tehuantepec where Playa Cangrejo is located is ground zero. The isthmus, the narrowest part of Mexico with the state of Oaxaca on the south side and Veracruz on the north side, was a central part of the 1976-1982 Jose Lopez-Portillo administration's Alpha Omega plan for a trade corridor. While that plan never was materialized, former president Ernesto Zedillo brought the idea back to life with his Megaproject plan for shrimp and eucalyptus farms and a dry canal through the isthmus. While some of the road building, land acquisition and industrial farming projects outlined in the Megaproject did take place, for the most part it also stagnated. But many NGO leaders and academics think that Fox's PPP, the latest incarnation of the dry canal idea, is dangerously close to becoming reality.

"Fox's PPP has been more successful in generating business interest in eight months than the PRI's[17] Megaproject was in five years," said Wendy Call, a journalist working in Matias Romero on a fellowship from the Institute of Current World Affairs, who works closely with activist Carlos Beas. "Fox has much more success with the World Bank and IMF than Zedillo did. He is heralded as the man who will bring global capitalism to Mexico."

Call said that the main factors driving Fox's PPP include his determination to facilitate the success of the FTAA; pressure from the U.S. to decrease Mexican migration, which would be achieved by jobs created along the dry canal; and the overall consolidation of power over land and people in the south of Mexico, including the effect this would have on the Zapatistas in Chiapas. The plan includes projects throughout Central America, specifically in Honduras, Guatemala and Nicaragua, largely designed for the benefit of Mexico.

"Fox's apparent assumption that he could just sell this plan to all of Central America shows his ignorance about Central America," she said. "He's treating Central Americans the same way the U.S. government has always treated Mexicans, saying 'We're here to save you from poverty and you need to go along with everything we say.'"

Oaxaca and the isthmus in particular is one of the poorest

states in Mexico and also the state with one of the highest indigenous populations. There are at least 56 indigenous groups in Oaxaca, including the Mixe, Mixteca, Zapotec and some groups of African descent. It is also one of the areas richest in bio-diversity. The Chimalapas jungle on the isthmus is judged to be even richer in bio-diversity and have more virgin forest than the famous Lacondon jungle in Chiapas. It is the source of 40 percent of the water for the whole country, with springs giving birth to countless rivers that feed coastal lagoons and empty into the Pacific.

Over 70 percent of the people in Oaxaca live in extreme poverty, and 30 percent of the population is indigenous.

While relatively few people in Mexico have heard of the PPP or know any details about it, it has become a hot topic in the international investment scene. At the June 15, 2001 "Concepcion Tuxtla" summit meeting of Central American presidents in San Salvador, the IDB announced its commitment to leading the search for funding for the project from the World Bank, the IMF, national banks and private corporations and investors.

Even as it was selling the plan to the international community, the government was mum about the plan within the country.

"A lot of people don't have any idea what the PPP is," said Elva Flores Muñoz of the Red de Derechos Humanos de Tepeyac (Tepeyac Human Rights Network) in Oaxaca. "State and federal government officials say we don't know what you're talking about, the project doesn't exist. But even journalists from other countries tell us they'd posed as investors to meet with government officials and were given all sorts of information about the project. If this is supposed to be beneficial, why aren't they informing the population about what it is?"

In 2003 Call wrote a report documenting the lack of community involvement in the PPP planning process. She noted that in 2002, in response to pressure from local groups and international NGOs, the IDB promised to make more efforts to inform and involve the public, including posting relevant information on their web site. But the results were far from impressive.[18]

"The only relevant document posted to the IDB website was a nine page summary," she wrote "Though the summary listed some budget figures and a few of the points to be connected by new or improved highways, the document was far too vague for any particular town or village in the region to know whether they might be directly affected by the construction."

Flores Muñoz noted that what little the government has told people about the plan has focused on the jobs that supposedly would be created. But she said that the better jobs would be skilled jobs, which wouldn't be open to most people from the isthmus, and overall the industrialization would destroy the way of life indigenous people have embraced for centuries.

"Salina Cruz is a clear example of what this project will do," said Flores Muñoz. "It was a fishing community until Pemex came in, and now everyone works for Pemex and it is one of the most polluted ports in the world."

The PPP will be facilitated by NAFTA, the FTAA and the controversial indigenous rights law passed by Fox and the Mexican Congress at the end of April, 2001 called COCOPA.[19] All of these policies and plans accelerate the trend of land privatization and multinational investment and exploitation of land and labor in Mexico and Central America, and the destruction of natural habitats and displacement of indigenous peoples.

Indigenous people and community leaders note that so far the PPP has been characterized by the same kind of manipulation, deception and misinformation used to push through NAFTA, COCOPA and the FTAA.

"Communities are also being asked to donate some of their land, being told the highway will benefit them," said Flores Muñoz. "People were thinking they could put up little stores by the highway and sell tortillas, walk their donkeys along the road. They don't realize this is a super-highway and they'll have no access to it."

Teodocio Angel Molina of UCIZONI noted that it is the government's longstanding paternalistic relationship with indigenous people that makes something like the PPP possible. By this he means the government's process of doling out or taking away land and favors from indigenous communities on a whim, playing communities against each other and keeping them ultimately all dependent on the government for survival. A clear example of this is in Chimalapas, where territory disputes between indigenous groups have festered since the Spanish entered the area to cut cedar in the 1600s. Over the past 40 years the government has continued to play people off each other in numerous territory conflicts between indigenous communities, and between indigenous people and mestizo (mixed race) cattle farmers, all complicated by an ongoing border dispute between Oaxaca and Chiapas.

Much of the land in the PPP proposed area still belongs to indigenous people, protected by long-standing Constitutional guarantees. The goal of the government is to wrest this land from communal, indigenous hands and put it into the hands of individuals, who then can be forced or persuaded to sell to the government or multinational corporations. Often the intermediate step in this process is to turn the land over to ejidos, collectively-run lands that are closer to individual control than the communal lands. The COCOPA "indigenous rights" law, which drew widespread protest from indigenous people throughout the country, failed to provide any meaningful protections for this land. In fact, the national law is a particular set-back to Oaxaca's state indigenous law, passed in 1995 after intense lobbying by indigenous rights groups, which provided more protections for indigenous people but can be superseded by the weaker national law.

"The goal of the government is to create division among

the communities so that the government can come in as the savior," said Cesar Morales Rodriguez of the campesino organization CAMPO.

While organizing resistance to the PPP has been a slow and difficult process, because of lack of available information, transportation and communication barriers and pressing local conflicts, UCIZONI and other groups have been fostering a growing awareness of and movement against the plan.

And right from the start, the resistance to the plan and to globalization as a whole has been met with extreme repression. UCIZONI members have received serious death threats and one was actually murdered near San Antonio. In 1999 in Oaxaca, the National Commission on Human Rights logged over 1,200 complaints about abuse from police and the military, including 225 illegal detentions, 331 cases of torture, 25 disappearances and 10 executions.[20] They say this repression is aimed mainly at quashing resistance.

"These are very rich lands, so there have been lots of invasions by big landowners supported by the government," said Sofia Robles of the indigenous group Servicios del Pueblo Mixe. "When the people defend their land, there is repression. They are jailed and attacked. The government is trying to destroy their organizing structures, and every day the communities are losing more and more territory."

The falling corn and coffee prices caused by NAFTA have also aided the government in their campaign of displacement, as farmers who can no longer make a living on the land are forced to migrate to cities in Mexico and the U.S. looking for work.

Meanwhile of all the havoc that will be wreaked by the PPP if its various facets are allowed to come to fruition, the imminent destruction of the Chimalapas rain forest and the indigenous communities that live there may be the most tragic and globally harmful. The project would open the jungle to sacking by the U.S., Canadian, Chilean and other lumber companies that are already invading the Lacondon and other areas.

From February through May 1998 the Chimalapas was ravaged by forest fires, which leveled hundreds of thousands of hectares, which will take 80-100 years to regenerate. Molina says that the fires coincided in time and location with proposed dam and road projects. And he remembers that not long before the fires started, UCIZONI had asked the government for 80,000 pesos (roughly $8,500) for five fire stations in the area, a request that was denied.

"We're convinced those fires were started on purpose," he said. "There are a lot of interests at work here."

The government has proposed creating a protected biosphere in the Chimalapas, but locals fear this move would actually fit into the government's overall plan of privatization and displacement. The Biosphere as the government has proposed it, Molina says, would be planned and controlled by outside academics and officials without any input from local populations, and the sole focus would be on the preservation of flora and fauna, not indigenous rights or cultures. In this way, the reserve would actually serve as a tool to further displace indigenous people from the jungle mirroring the situation currently playing out in Montes Azules, Chiapas. UCIZONI and other organizations have made a counter-proposal for a Campesino Reserve, which would protect indigenous people as well as plants and animals, and which would be management by local communal processes.

So far the government has refused to accept the Campesino Reserve plan, according to Molina, "because that would be one step toward autonomy, and that would set a dangerous precedent."

When the puzzle that includes pieces called the PPP, NAFTA, the FTAA and COCOPA is finished, many fear it will be a far different Mexico from the one they know and love. A Mexico where fishermen like Martinez are forced to migrate to the cities, and where indigenous campesinos are forced to immigrate to the U.S. A Mexico where logging companies shave the lush hills of the Chimalapas rain forest, and oil companies soil the sparkling sea.

But thanks to the efforts of local organizers and the international activist community, grassroots resistance against the plan continues to grow.

Call's report notes that, "Many of the participants in the civil society-organized July 2003 international forum on the PPP [in Managua, Nicaragua] signed a 'Manifesto Against the IDB.' Since then, the statement has been circulating through activist networks and on the Internet."

Columbus Day 2003 (Oct. 12) was declared a continental day of action against the PPP, with 60,000 people in North and South America protesting against the plan.[21] UCIZONI organized a protest in which over 1,000 people blocked the Trans-Isthmus highway in Oaxaca.[22]

"This is all part of a very aggressive process, the same process that gives us Plan Colombia, that gives us new U.S. military bases in Ecuador, that gives us bombing exercises in Vieques,"[23] said UCIZONI leader Beas. "The black color of the oil from Pemex is symbolic of the exploitation of the people. We are up against a monster that is putting the very life of our planet in danger."

For more information:

Mexico Solidarity Network, www.mexicosolidarity.org.

Action for Social and Ecological Justice: http://www.asej.org/ACERCA/ppp.

A little girl in the Nuevo San Isidro community in Montes Azules, Chiapas, where the government and conservation organizations are trying to force people to leave the jungle. Photo by Kari Lydersen.

A radio provides one of the only links with the outside world in Montes Azules. Photo by Kari Lydersen.

# CHAPTER TWO

# Who is Destroying the Jungle?
## Politics and Preservation in Montes Azules, Chiapas

A flash of lightning silhouettes the wiry figure of Joseu Jimenez Cruz as he raises his fist to make a point.

"We want our new generation of kids to be able to see all the different kinds of animals and trees here," he said, as smoke wafted around his body from a nearby campfire and a mangy dog sniffed his high mud-caked rubber boots. "We are conserving these plants and animals so our children will know them. We are taking care of our mother earth."

Sheets of tropical rain pound on the thatch roof of the open air hut where Jimenez and his family prepare their food on this evening in August 2003, in the Nuevo San Rafael community of indigenous Chol people in the Montes Azules region of the Lacandon rain forest in Chiapas, Mexico.

Jimenez and the other 60-some members of the community, also known as Ignacio Allende, have only been here a year and a half. They came because, as supporters of the EZLN army (Ejercito Zapatista de Liberación Nacional—better known as the Zapatistas), they were being terrorized by members of the Paz y Justicia paramilitary group in their home community of El Calvario. A little boy who huddles by Jimenez's legs saw his father murdered by Paz y Justicia in January 1998. Around that same time a woman was raped by the paramilitary group.

Because of this ongoing violence from the paramilitaries, Jimenez and his compañeros struck out to find a new home in the jungle, where the Zapatista movement was born. The group tried living in two other locations, where they weren't able to grow food, before ending up in Nuevo San Rafael, which is separated from the nearest gravel road by a 45 minute hike through jungle and pastureland, and a canoe ride across the muddy Lacantun River.

Now they have built a community of thatch-roof huts and open air kitchens and live a sustainable existence growing corn and coffee.

But along with many other communities in the region, they are in a critical struggle to hold onto their land. The government is trying to oust most of the Chol, Tsotsil, Tseltal and Tojolabal indigenous communities that call Montes Azules home. Their stated reasons are two-fold—that the land is a federally protected biosphere, and that the land belongs to a group called the Lacondon Indians, whom other indigenous people refer to as the "so-called Lacondones" since they are actually not originally from the area. The local communities under siege think the government's real reasons for wanting them out have more to do with the ongoing counter-insurgency effort against the Zapatistas, and the move to open the area up to foreign investment, including research by pharmaceutical companies; development by eco-tourism outfits; the establishment of hydro-electric power plants and the extraction of lumber, oil, uranium and fresh water.

Besides the fact that they need land and homes where they can survive free from paramilitary violence, part of the reason the indigenous communities are determined to stay in Montes Azules is to guard the jungle from this type of exploitation by foreign companies and others with an interest in its rich natural resources.

Protecting Chiapas from exploitation by foreigners is one of the primary platforms of the Zapatista movement, and many (though not all) of the communities slated for removal are Zapatista-aligned. In 1995 the federal government began heavy militarization in the jungle, and this militarization has been increased recently. In early 2003, coinciding with the start of the U.S.'s invasion of Iraq, the Mexican Navy began patrols on the Usumacinta River which borders the Lacandon, supposedly to prevent terrorists from entering the country from Guatemala.[24]

The Lacandon, along with the nearby Chimalapas rainforest, is often described as the third most bio-diverse region in the world behind Indonesia and the Amazon River Basin.    It is home to one third of Mexico's bird species, one quarter of its animal species and almost half its butterfly species. It is also one of the world's primary sources of fresh water, and it is rich in oil and uranium.

About 80 percent of the Lacandon has already been destroyed by logging of its precious mahogany, cedar and other hardwoods that started in the 1800s, providing wood for expensive furniture for the wealthy elite of Spain, Mexico, England and the U.S.[25]

After the timber companies had taken all they could from large swaths of the jungle, cattle ranchers moved in to make use of the deforested land, further clearing it for grazing. As the rainforest tried to reclaim the land, ranchers used pesticide to kill the so-called "bad weeds" that were springing up. After several cycles of pesticide use, much of the soil became so devoid of nutrients that not even enough grass grows to support cattle grazing anymore.

"The World Bank promoted cattle ranching all over the world in the 1960s and '70s," said Miguel Angel Garcia, coordinator of the group Maderas del Pueblo (Trees of the People), which works to conserve the Chimalapas and Lacandon rainforests. "The beef produced here is destined for urban areas in central Mexico. Many indigenous people were convinced that cattle ranching was the way to go, that it was progress to turn jungle into pastureland. But now there are large areas of pasture without cattle, because the soil is so poor. And the forest has been destroyed."

The Mexican government actually encouraged many indigenous people to move to the jungle to do cattle ranching.

Then, as part of the agrarian reform process, indigenous people living in the Lacandon were allowed to petition for legal title to their land. As of 1972, 47 communities had filed for title to the land; with 17 having been awarded titles and 30 others still caught up in the bureaucratic process.[26]

In 1971 three communities of ("so-called") Lacandon Indians, numbering about 400 people total, were among those who filed for legal title. They asked for a total of 10,000 hectares. But to their surprise, while most of the claims took years to process, just eight months after filing the Lacandones were awarded a total of 614,321 hectares, about 1.2 million acres, or a third of the whole 1.8 million hectare Lacandon jungle.[27]

"It was like they won the lottery without even buying a ticket," says a booklet put out by Maderas del Pueblo.[28]

In 1978 the government declared 331,200 hectares of the Lacandon as the federally protected Montes Azules bio reserve, with about 70 percent of the reserve covering land that had been awarded to the Lacandon Indians. The area awarded to the Lacandon also included many of the other communities, including those who had and had not yet been given legal title to their land. In the last few years a number of new communities like Nuevo San Rafael have also been created within the area supposedly owned by the Lacandon. Other indigenous communities are outside Lacandon Indian territory but within the Montes Azules reserve. Besides the communities aligned with the Zapatistas, others are aligned with the long-time ruling PRI party and still others with ARIC-Independiente, an organization which typically sides with the moderate-left PRD party.

According to the U.S.-based group Conservation International, there are 225 communities in the protected area of Montes Azules. Thirty-two of these, mainly ones sympathetic to the Zapatistas, have been declared to be "illegal."

Conservation International and other U.S.-based groups, along with the Mexican government, blame these communities for "destroying" the rain forest. The government has issued orders for the removal of at least 21 communities, and locals estimate there are about 60 communities pegged for eviction.[29]

Conservation International has worked with the government to do aerial surveillance of the region and advocate for the removal of the "invading" communities. Community residents and activists in San Cristobal de las Casas, the international nerve center of Zapatista solidarity, blame Conservation International and other U.S. conservation groups for abetting the government in its counter-insurgency campaign. Representatives of the Mexico office of Conservation International did not return messages, but a U.S. spokesperson for the group, who asked not to be named, stressed that while Conservation International does want the indigenous people out of Montes Azules, they also plan to work with them to develop alternative communities and forms of sustenance. Jimenez said that on May 8, 2002, representatives from the federal government offered the residents of Nuevo San Rafael 100,000 pesos (about $10,000 US) to leave the land, but they refused.

"We don't want money, we want the land," he said. "The government dispenses gifts, like a kilo of maseca, a kilo of sugar, a liter of oil. But we don't want gifts, we want the land."

Nuevo San Rafael and the other communities under threat of expulsion are under constant pressure from the government and the Lacandones to vacate the land. They frequently receive visits from Lacandones armed with machetes and guns, and often the Lacandones are accompanied by members of the Navy or government officials from PROFEPA[30], the attorney general's office in charge of the environment, or SEMARNAP,[31] Mexico's department of the environment, natural resources and fisheries. The Lacandon come across the Lacantun River in large canoe-like boats often carved out of mahogany trees, similar to the canoes the other indigenous communities use, except the Lacandones' boats have motors. Sometimes they come in Navy boats.

Community members said that on April 12, 2003, three boatloads of armed Lacandones landed in Nuevo San Rafael and threatened the community that they had to be gone in 15 days. They also stole a $4,000 video camera from visiting indigenous video-makers with the Chiapas Media Project, which has offices in San Cristobal and Chicago. Jimenez says that a government PROFEPA official and Navy members were present during the robbery and did nothing to stop it. The community has filed a complaint with the courts regarding the incident, but nothing has happened yet.

"It was 2:30 p.m. when they entered the community," says a written report about the incident. "They all entered but three Lacandones were the most aggressive. They said we had to leave these lands, they had firearms and one fat Lacandon had tear gas. The majority brought machetes. They didn't respect us and they verbally assaulted a group of human rights observers who had arrived that day. The Lacandones said we had 15 days to leave the land. The government officials stayed back and didn't say anything."

The report also describes harassment and intimidation suffered by the nearby Nuevo San Isidro community, a Tsotsil community which has been there only six months after fleeing paramilitary violence in their home community of Chavageval.

The same day the Lacandones stole the video camera, they also paid a visit to Nuevo San Isidro and told the community to be gone in eight days. Again, government officials were present "and did nothing to calm the aggression of the Lacandones," says the report.

These menacing visits to both communities continued throughout the spring and summer.

For example on April 25, 2003, two Lacandones accompanied by 11 Navy soldiers, a PROFEPA rep and another government official entered Nuevo San Rafael and threatened them, and on April 27, the community was invaded by nine armed Lacandones who came in Navy boats along with Navy members.

During a visit Jimenez and his 16-year-old daughter Maricela made to Nuevo San Isidro in July 2003, the community members gathered in a dirt-floored, thatch-roofed school house to discuss the intimidation they are suffering. A young man named Alfredo read painstakingly from a handwritten log the community was keeping of Lacandon activity.

"The Lacandones said if the government doesn't solve this problem, they will do whatever they want," said Alfredo.

The government has told the different indigenous communities that it will mediate discussions between them and the Lacandones. But since the government has obviously been supporting the Lacandones, the communities scoff at the suggestion that it could be a neutral mediator. The Zapatista-aligned communities have said they will not dialogue with the government until it honors the San Andres Peace Accords, which were negotiated between the government and the Zapatistas in 1996 but never implemented.

"The government has the mentality that they can do whatever they want, but we won't stand for that," said Jimenez, 38.

In April 2003 the 32 communities slated for removal filed a complaint with the Inter-American Commission on Human Rights, arguing that among other things their rights to the land are protected by Convention 169 of the International Labour Organization treaty, which Mexico has signed.[32]

Meanwhile there are various inconsistencies in the awarding of land to the Lacandones, even besides the fact that about 66 Lacandon families were given so much of the jungle while about 4,000 other indigenous families were given nothing. For one thing, two of the three communities where the Lacandones live were outside the boundaries of the land they were given. In

1985 the government extended their holdings even more to include these communities.

The original Lacandon Indians were all killed by Spanish conquistadors after putting up what is often described as a valiant, centuries-long struggle. The last two known "real" Lacandones are said to have died in a Guatemalan prison in 1712.[33] The Indians now known as the Lacandon, or "so-called Lacandon," are Mayans who originally lived on the Yucatan peninsula and migrated to the Lacandon in the 1700s. They are also known as Caribes, since they originally come from the Caribbean.

However with the government's blessing the "so-called Lacandon" have eagerly taken on the role of the ancestral inheritors of the Lacandon jungle, even capitalizing on this identity to run various tourist operations.

In 1974 the Lacandon signed a contract with a quasi-governmental company called COFOLASA for the logging of 35,000 cubic meters of wood per year.[34]

"It's a lie that these Lacandones are the ancestral owners of the jungle," said Garcia, who also worked as an advisor on indigenous affairs to the government before being fired for 'disloyalty,' he said. "The government needed an intermediary who would let them extract wood from the jungle, and the other communities wouldn't let them do this, but the Caribes (Lacandones) would. Now the Lacandones run all kinds of tourist outfits, they have all these signs in English saying 'Historic cornfield this way' or 'Ancient temple that way.' Most of the young people speak English instead of Mayan to work as tour guides. Everything they do is fake."

In addition to cash for the logging contract, the government has reportedly also given the Lacandones gifts such as a small airplane and SUVs.

"Historically in the jungle there have always been disputes between different indigenous groups," said a man named Elizeo, a leader of the group CIEPAC, the San Cristobal-based

Economic and Political Investigative Center for Community Action. "But the government is manipulating these conflicts and manipulating the famous so-called Lacandones so it can exploit natural resources."

Eco-tourism of the type run by the Lacandones is one of the reasons so many parties have their sights set on the jungle. Throughout Latin America, there has been much controversy over operations that claim to be ecologically friendly but are really more or less regular hotels with some "green-washing" thrown in.

A good example of this dichotomy was the 2002 Isuzu Challenge "Ruta Maya" (Mayan Route), which featured a caravan of SUVs painted with tiger stripes barreling through the jungle in the name of rainforest preservation.[35]

The event, which is held in a different remote location every year, billed itself as part of "the struggle against illegal deforestation and tree theft that exploits the largely isolated areas of the forest for the chopping and stealing of rare and expensive trees."

The event web site also notes that the Isuzu Challenge "contributed cellular and satellite systems to aid the forest rangers and local authorities in searching, locating and preventing tree theft."

However many local indigenous residents saw it as a "Challenge" to their sovereignty and peace, and as another example of foreign incursion into the Lacandon. (NGO leaders also note wryly that one of the challenge participants was Israeli General Avihu Ben Nun, a key figure in the first Gulf War and hardly a known environmentalist).

The Isuzu Challenge participants stayed at Rancho Esmeralda, an eco-tourism lodge that has also been a point of contention in the region. In March 2003 Rancho Esmeralda owners Ellen Jones and Glenn Wersch left the area, saying they were forced out by the Zapatistas. The couple said they were forced to leave on Feb. 28, 2003, two months after they first reported to the government that they were being threatened by Zapatistas in the nearby communities of Nuevo Jerusalen and the municipality 1 de enero. "At 7 a.m. about 100 men armed with machetes began to gather at the ranch entrance," says a press release on their behalf. "When Glenn Wersch returned from the town he was attacked by a mob of Zapatistas hurling rocks and trying to stop his vehicle and grab him."[36]

The ranch has now been taken over by Zapatistas, who maintain that while they didn't force Jones and Wersch to leave, the land where the ranch is located belongs intrinsically to the indigenous people, not a foreign entrepreneur.

While Rancho Esmeralda is no longer operating, Garcia notes that there are numerous other eco-tourism projects in the works, including luxury operations with five-star hotels.

Construction has already been started on a major hotel complex in Lacanja Chansayab, built by the company Gerardo Turrent-Inmobiliaria San Martin. On Dec. 17, 2002 the Chiapas secretary of tourism also announced plans for resorts built by other large companies including Xcaret and Xel-ha. Xcaret has already drawn intense criticism for the environmental impact of one of its resorts in Cancun.[37]

Along with eco-tourism, indigenous leaders and advocates are also concerned about what is often termed bio-prospecting, or more critically, bio-piracy. An influx of scientists and representatives of pharmaceutical companies are researching the curative properties of local flora and fauna, and indigenous people's knowledge of them, with the intention of patenting their discoveries for marketing.

Indigenous communities are afraid that large-scale research in the Lacandon will eventually destroy the environment and displace their communities, and they know they will get little or no benefit from whatever discoveries are made. Already there is a biological research station in the Chajul area of Montes Azules sponsored by Conservation International and the Mexican organization Espacios Naturales y Desarolla

Sustenable AC. Garcia notes that another research station funded partly by the Ford Motor Co. is also under construction in the Rio Tzendales area, though a legal complaint has been filed seeking to halt its development.[38]

Two of the companies which have an interest in research in the jungle are the large Mexican biotech firm Grupo Pulsar and the San Diego, Calif.-based company Diversa, which has come under fire for its plans to patent microbes at Yellowstone National Park.[39] Diversa actually had a contract with the government to do research in Montes Azules, but it was canceled due to local pressure.

In a local news article, government officials said that while they respect the rights of people legally living in Montes Azules, since the Zapatista uprising of 1994 the area has seen many "invasions" by indigenous groups which are harming the environment. Officials quoted in news reports noted that the jungle plays a crucial role in regulating the climate and is home to rare species such as the guacamaya bird and the white tortoise. They said that each new home built by "invaders"—displaced peoples indigenous to the region but new to specific plots of land— represents the loss of 10,500 plants and the disappearance of species.[40]

Indigenous residents counter that the building of tourist outfits, research stations and other operations supported by the government causes far more upheaval in the jungle than the simple, sustainable indigenous communities.

"They say we are destroying the rainforest, but it is the opposite," said Jimenez. "The multinational companies are destroying the rainforest. We are protectors of the rainforest. It is part of our way of life. We are the friends of the jungle."

The government has in fact promised to give new land to the communities it is trying to get out of Montes Azules. But most aren't buying it. Some communities which have voluntarily left the land already have ended up as refugees.

Jimenez and many other indigenous people feel that the

way things normally go in Mexico, if the government gets them off the land it will be free to carry on with the tourism, bio-prospecting, hydro-electric energy and other projects it has planned, and they will be thrown to the wind, without land or homes once again.

If they are displaced from the jungle, after having previously been uprooted from their home communities in different parts of Chiapas, they fear they will join the ranks of indigenous people who are no longer able to make a living on the land at all. They are likely to be forced into the industrial workforce, ending up toiling in maquilas in Mexico City or along the U.S.-Mexico border.

"Many businesses also have an interest in exploiting and utilizing the displaced indigenous populations as cheap labor for maquilas," says a report from a Zapatista organization.

However since these maquila jobs are disappearing as well, going to Asia where wages are even lower, there's a good chance they won't be able to make it in the maquila zones either. In that case their only choice may be to take the huge risks involved in crossing illegally into the United States, splitting up their families and abandoning their culture along the way.

Marcelo Mendez Guzman, a member of the Red de Defensores human rights network from the Palenque area of the Lacandon, noted that many of his family members have already moved to the U.S., and that there are whole towns in his region with no men because they have all gone to the U.S. in search of work.

"Many people are migrating out; the youths are going to Cancun, Guadalajara and the majority to the U.S.," he said. "In my community of about 1,500, 20 young people have already gone to the U.S. and a lot more are talking about it. It has changed the community a lot."

Before the mid-1990s there was very little immigration from southern Mexico to the border or the U.S., but today immigrants from Chiapas and the neighboring states of Oaxaca and Veracruz make up a large portion of the migration to border cities and U.S. cities like San Francisco and Chicago.[41]

"This can all be understood as part of the process of globalization," said human rights worker Elizeo. "Chiapas is a strategic zone for implementation of Plan Puebla-Panama and other mega-projects and designs the government has with multinational companies."

When these projects come in, many of the people will have to go.

The residents of Montes Azules are struggling to hold on not only to their homes in the jungle but to their very ways of life.

For more information:

Global Exchange:

www.globalexchange.org/countries/mexico/biodiversity.

Thousands protested against the FTAA (ALCA in Spanish) in Quito in October 2002. Photo by Allan Gomez.

A store in Guayaquil, Ecuador celebrates the country's switch to the U.S. dollar as its official currency. Photo by Kari Lydersen.

# CHAPTER THREE

# Ecuador and the Almighty Dollar

A chain of "dollar stores" in malls and on crowded downtown streets in Guayaquil, Ecuador's largest city, sport large red, white, blue and green signs—a U.S. dollar bill with George Washington's face. The "O" in the word "dolarazo" is smiling rakishly and wearing an Uncle Sam hat.

The signs aren't just advertising an eclectic variety of goods for a dollar, but the very fact that Ecuador, a country of 12.9 million located right on the equator in South America, now uses the U.S. dollar instead of sucres as its official currency.

The greenbacks on the sign might be grinning, but dollarization hasn't exactly brought smiles to the vast majority of people in Ecuador. Since the U.S. dollar—the very same bills people use in the U.S.—became the official currency for Ecuador on Sept. 12, 2000, prices for many consumer goods are equivalent to prices in the U.S.: $1 for a gallon of gas, $12 for a CD, $30 for a brand name shirt, 60 cents for a Coke. Housing and food prices are less than in the U.S., but still not cheap. Yet the average Ecuadorian worker makes only $4 to $6 a day. The national census puts average wages for the service industry at $3,383 a year, and the bulk of people working in part-time jobs or the informal economy earn much less.[42]

Official figures put unemployment between 8 and 15 percent from 1998 to 2003, but the number of people not earning a living is much higher.[43] About 70 percent of the population are considered either unemployed or underemployed, and most working people support multiple family members who are unemployed. Many people make their living selling candy or water on buses or the streets for tiny profits.

Dollarization was instituted despite the fact that former president Jamil Mahuad was deposed on January 21, 2000 by thousands of indigenous people, workers and military leaders protesting his dollarization plan.

After a military and indigenous coalition invaded the Congress building and forced Mahuad from power, a triumvirate junta was formed between Antonio Vargas, president of the powerful indigenous organization CONAIE (Confederation of Indigenous Nationalities of Ecuador); former Supreme Court justice Carlos Solorzano; and Armed Forces Chief Carlos Mendoza, following the leadership of Colonel Lucio Gutierrez. They declared a "Parliament for the People" and vowed to end poverty and the rampant governmental corruption that has long plagued the country.

But the coup proved to be short-lived, as the next day the military wing withdrew support from the indigenous movement and ceded power to vice president Gustavo Noboa, essentially handing power back to the same government that had been deposed. Many Ecuadorians feel certain that orders and threats of sanctions from the U.S. were behind this move. Despite ongoing protest, Noboa went through with the dollarization plan, signing the bill on March 9, 2000. Dollarization was intended to yank Ecuador out of a downward spiral of inflation and devaluation—the sucre had lost 67 percent of its value in 1999 and logged an inflation rate as high as 104 percent a year, the highest in Latin America. The government defaulted on much of its foreign debts in 1999, and the country was forced to adhere to IMF austerity measures to obtain a $300 million loan approved in the spring of 2000, part of a U.S.-backed $2 billion plan for international aid.

Inflation has in fact been curtailed substantially through dollarization—in August 2000 inflation was down to 1.4 percent, from 14.3 percent in January.

Even so, since dollarization took effect the worst fears of the populace are well on their way to being realized. Ecuadorians say that poverty has increased, with the attendant crime and violence in its wake. Wages are generally similar to what they were before dollarization, when there were 25,000 sucres to the dollar. But prices are pegged to the dollar rather than the sucre.

During a visit in December 2001, Gustavo Peralta, a Guayaquil resident who used to work for the city's main beer company, noted that an employer can tell his workers they should be happy with $4 a day, since that would have been equivalent to a livable wage of 100,000 sucres. But $4 today buys far less than 100,000 sucres did before dollarization. Prices are generally rounded up to the dollar, so things that cost the equivalent of 20 or 30 cents before might be a whole dollar now.

"You used to be able to prepare a meal for a family for 10,000 sucres," said Betsy Peralta, Gustavo's daughter. "Now it takes several dollars. The price of everything has gone up."

David Turner, a Quito resident and former staffer for the indigenous organization CONAIE, said incomes have plummeted since dollarization.

"Dollarization is a trick," said Turner, a British native with a long white ponytail. "The bankers and other speculators in cahoots with the government had managed to bring the sucre down from 5,000 to the dollar to 25,000 in the last four months of 1999...so someone making a monthly salary worth $200 when the sucre was worth 5,000 to the dollar ended up being paid $40 when the sucre was converted to the dollar at 25,000."

Many workers in Quito make only $40 a month, he noted, while even professionals make only about $100 a month. Public sector employees such as teachers and healthcare workers were hardest hit by dollarization, since their income was calculated solely in sucres while employees of multinational companies have always had incomes more closely pegged to the dollar.

As part of its austerity measures, the IMF encouraged Ecuador not to raise its minimum wage. The IMF also succeeded in pushing Congress to increase the "value added tax," or sales tax, by two percentage points, a move that makes the already rising price of essential goods even higher. As in the U.S., the sales tax is a regressive tax that hits poorer people harder since they spend a higher percentage of their income on necessities than do the wealthy, who are able to save a greater portion of their income. Revenue could also have been raised by programs that taxed the wealthy in equal proportions, like a progressive income tax, but as in other countries this was not the route the IMF chose to take.

Residents of Guayaquil and Quito live in constant fear of crime, always a serious problem, which has gotten much worse since dollarization. Carjackings and muggings in broad daylight are common, as are armed robberies and rampant pick-pocketing and purse snatching. Betsy Peralta always carries the smallest purse possible to avoid attracting attention, and she never goes out after dark if she can help it, especially since she was nearly car-jacked in broad daylight.

In Quito and other northern areas, crime and general economic problems are compounded by the influx of Colombian refugees fleeing the U.S.-funded civil war in Colombia. "There is much more crime," said Turner. "And it's not just criminals, but 'honorable' people. I know people who have gotten robbed and the robbers give them their papers (documents) back, or $5 back to get home. People are just doing this because they need the money." Dollarization has also spurred an increase in immigration, with Ecuadorians fleeing out of the country to Spain or other European countries, or whenever possible, to the U.S. There are now at least 1.5 million Ecuadorians working legally or illegally abroad,[44] and money sent back to Ecuador from foreign countries is an essential part of the economy.

As it gets more difficult for farmers to make a living, there is also an internal migration from the country to miserable slums in the cities.

"People are leaving in waves," said Monica Chuy, an indigenous activist from the Lago Agrio region along the Colombian border who now lives in Quito and works with an indigenous media project. "Not just from the city but from the campo (the country)."

The U.S. government was a major proponent of the dollarization plan all along. Two days before Noboa signed dollarization into law, Robert McTeeter of the Dallas Federal Reserve Bank endorsed dollarization, and numerous U.S. Congressmen spoke in favor of it. The Senate Joint Economics Committee also published a series of pamphlets in Spanish with names like Basics of Dollarization and the Citizens' Guide to Dollarization. Former Sen. Connie Mack (R-Fla.), then-chairman of the Joint Economics Committee, introduced a dollarization incentive bill called the International Monetary Stability Act allowing the Treasury Department to rebate 85 percent of the profit it gets from printing dollars that are sold to other countries.

Dollarization means that interest rates are set by the U.S. Federal Reserve, even if the Ecuadorian economy is going in the opposite direction.[45] U.S.-based and other multinational companies benefit from dollarization because it makes foreign investment more stable and attractive. There is substantial foreign investment in Ecuador, including by oil, banana and lumber companies.

"This is clearly a bonanza for employers," said Turner. "They only have to pay their employees 20 percent of what they would have had to pay before the sucre went up from 5,000 to the dollar [to 25,000 to the dollar, as described earlier]. This is true particularly for exporters of bananas and other goods whose workers' wages went down while they continue to sell on a relatively stable international market."

Meanwhile even after Noboa was instated, protests against dollarization and other economic "reforms" including the privatization of state industries continued. A week after Congress

Monica Chuy and David Turner, pictured with their son, work with the indigenous organization CONAIE in Quito. Photo by Kari Lydersen.

approved dollarization, the country's largest confederation of unions staged massive peaceful protests and strikes in Quito.

Several weeks later, farmers carried out a strike protesting dollarization and the proposed privatization of the Farm Social Security program.

In January 2001, the anniversary of the coup, CONAIE started a series of roadblocks and protests against steep hikes in gas and oil prices and bus fares that Noboa had passed in late December in keeping with IMF demands. By Jan. 24, 2001 the military moved on the roadblocks, and four indigenous activists were injured. Protests also broke out on university campuses, and about 8,000 indigenous and student activists occupied the campus of the Salesian Polytechnic University in Quito. On Feb. 2 Noboa declared a state of emergency, giving the government power to search people at roadblocks and to search activists' homes. Six indigenous people were killed in the uprising.[46]

Today, CONAIE and other community and indigenous groups continue to organize and gear up for new campaigns against the effects of dollarization and globalization. Graffiti blanketing Quito and Guayaquil denounces the proposed privatization of electricity and education; Plan Colombia and the U.S.'s role in it; and the Bush and Noboa administrations in general. There is even substantial graffiti decrying the war in Afghanistan.

As the first country besides U.S. territories and small islands to dollarize, Ecuador's fate is a harbinger of things to come.

The IMF, the U.S. and other foreign interests will likely push widespread dollarization as a solution to the continent's economic woes, and an aid to globalization and free trade. Argentina's peso had already been pegged one to one to the dollar, one of the issues that brought the people's wrath down upon former president Fernando de la Rua, who was deposed in December 2001 in the wake of massive rioting and protest.

At a June 1999 meeting of the IMF in Washington D.C., speakers discussed the possibilities of widespread dollarization in Latin America, defining dollarization as the adoption of another country's currency be it the U.S. dollar, euro or yen. The IMF said the risks of dollarization include loss of seignorage profits (the profits from printing money) and loss of monetary independence, but noted the "longer-term benefits of increasing economic financial integration into a broader regional and global economy."

IMF plans didn't pan out well for Argentina, which went through four presidents in two months as protests left at least 27 dead and banks and foreign businesses collapsed. Many blamed the financial crisis on the pegging of the Argentine peso to the U.S. dollar. Turner said Ecuadorians watched these events with apprehension, aware of the similarities in the two countries' economic situations.

"Even pro-dollarization economists here as elsewhere are looking nervously at the financial melt-down in Argentina, a country that Ecuador's present policies have in part been modeled on," said Turner (in December 2001, as these events unfolded).

"Dollarization is like trying to lose weight by wiring your mouth shut," Ramiro Crespo, president of a Quito brokerage firm, told *The Miami Herald.* "It's a desperate measure."[47]

As in Argentina, Ecuadorians feel they are between a rock and a hard place, with harsh austerity measures imposed by the IMF from abroad, and a corrupt government at home.

"It's the same story in many parts of the world," said Turner. "Where the IMF, the World Bank and other bodies control small, impoverished economies and demand 'structural' economic changes while overlooking the social and economic consequences to the poor."

In October 2002 Ecuador became an international battleground over globalization, as tens of thousands of indigenous people, union members and international activists protested in Quito during a trade ministerial about the FTAA.

"It was really inspiring to see the number of people who came from so far away, and from neighboring Latin American countries like Peru and Bolivia," said Allan Gomez, an Ecuadorian activist and radio producer who lives in Chicago. "It was the result of a lot of organizing, but it also showed how high awareness of ALCA (Spanish acronym for the FTAA) and its effects already is in Latin America. It's a whole different story than in the U.S. The media coverage there was completely anti-ALCA and in favor of the protests, as opposed to protests in the U.S."

In the ensuing years dissatisfaction about dollarization and the effects of globalization in the country have only grown. When populist military leader Lucio Gutierrez was elected president in November 2002, many Ecuadorians were hopeful that the concerns of the poor and indigenous would take center stage.

And he has made efforts to protect their rights. For example at *The Miami Herald*'s annual Americas Conference in Coral Gables, Fla. in October 2003,[48] Gutierrez demanded that the U.S. do away with unbalanced agricultural subsidies and that free trade agreements take into account the needs of developing countries. But anti-globalization and indigenous activists say the majority of the population is just as impoverished as before, and they have been disappointed in Gutierrez's overall support for free trade policies, including the FTAA.

"Movements to oust Gutierrez are already underway," noted Gomez. "And it's clear that the real numbers and real power are going to come from the indigenous people. I think the non-indigenous people in Ecuador are becoming conscious of that."

For more information: CONAIE, http://conaie.org

Boys in the Montaña de la Flor community, which has been displaced numerous times in land ownership disputes. Photo by Kari Lydersen.

A boy stands in the wreckage of his home in the "20 de abril" community in Honduras. Photo by Kari Lydersen.

# CHAPTER FOUR

# From the Mountains to the Sea
## The Fight for Land in Honduras

O*n a humid day in April 2002 about 40 members of the San Juan Bautista Garifuna community gather under one of the few remaining trees in a dirt lot next to the emerald waters of the Atlantic, on the north coast of Honduras that their people have occupied for over 200 years.*

*Suddenly, a spark seems to run through the crowd: there are pointed glances and quick exchanges in their native language, and the teenage boys instinctively slide to the outer edges of the group, standing relaxed but at attention, machetes that moments earlier blended seamlessly with their U.S.-style clothing now held prominently in view. Some of them dash off to shrubbery at the side of the field and come back with sturdy branches—potential weapons—in hand. Some of the older women do the same, moving slightly slower but with no less agility or determined strength...*

Scenes like this are part of the fabric of life for the Garifuna community, people of African descent who came to the Atlantic coast of Honduras after being shuttled around various island territories by the French, English and Spanish.

The Garifuna originated with Africans on Spanish slave ships who ended up landing or wrecking on San Vicente island in the mid-1600s. From there they moved to surrounding Caribbean islands and intermarried with local Caribbean people and Europeans. They became successful farmers and warriors, later aiding the French in attempting to fight off English invaders. But they were eventually defeated and the British exiled about 5,000 Garifuna to the island of Balliceau, where many died of yellow fever and hunger. Those who survived were brought to the Honduran port of Trujillo in 1797, and many made their way to Belize, Guatemala and Nicaragua. Today there are about 100,000 Garifuna in Honduras, as well as large diaspora populations in U.S. cities including Miami, New Orleans and New York.

In 1937 the Honduran government tried to roust the Garifuna community from San Juan, killing 25 and causing many others to flee. But despite the massacre the community survived, and they have been in an ongoing struggle to hold on to their territory ever since.

Today, they are fighting an army of would-be developers and tourism outfits, who would like to see the idyllic coast lined with five-star hotels, diving operations and safely contained examples of the "warm and colorful" Garifuna people as advertised in a guide circulated to business travelers at the airport.

On this afternoon, it turns out the police have been called by someone connected to Saturnina Jeronimo Martinez, the woman who owns these nine hectares of land, or National Party Senator Dario Munguia, who Martinez is selling the land to for a reported $3.8 million U.S. Martinez was given the land by the municipality in January 2002, as part of 63 hectares that were awarded to Garifuna people in response to their request for legal title to 328 hectares of traditional land. Once Munguia buys the land, the community fears, it will soon be turned into a hotel or resort. Nearby, in the Triunfa de la Cruz Garifuna community, a resort called Marbella stands half-built, a monument of both victory and foreboding. The Garifuna stalled the construction of the resort about five years ago through legal challenges. But they know they will not always be so lucky.

One of the poorest countries in Latin America, there is so far relatively little large-scale tourism in mainland Honduras. But still suffering the effects of Hurricane Mitch in 1998 as well as an ongoing drought and a legacy of international debt as old as the country itself, the government and speculators are desperate for profit. And anyone who has seen the lovely sunsets or swum in the warm waters of the Atlantic coast would find them hard to resist, including major resort developers and their potential guests.

The Honduran Constitution, specifically Article 107, protects the land rights of indigenous people (the Garifuna are generally considered to be indigenous). The article stipulates that a foreign company cannot own land within 40 kilometers of the coast. [49] Honduras is also supposed to be bound by Convention 169 of the International Labour Organization, which the country signed in 1995.[50] The Convention, which was also ratified by Mexico, Argentina, Norway and other countries, gives indigenous people strong rights to their traditional land as well as a say in how the land is used and a share of any profits from the land. But the Honduran government, notorious for its corruption, has both ignored the Convention and Constitution and found ways to get around them.

For example, Saturnina Martinez, the woman who owns the nine hectares, is Garifuna but leaders of the San Juan community say she is not from the area and that she has a history from other areas of acting as a middle-person in selling land to outsiders.

"The government will buy out indigenous people who don't represent the community or have any contact with the grassroots level, and claim they are acting on behalf of the indigenous people," said Nathan Pravia, president of the indigenous organization CONPAH.[51] "CONPAH is resisting these projects that we know won't benefit indigenous people, so the government wants to undermine us and replace us with their own indigenous leaders."

In Garifuna and other indigenous areas, the government has also used the tactic of declaring areas protected forest preserves in order to wrest them from indigenous and campesino control, then use them for whatever they please. This strategy has been used in Triunfa de la Cruz, where a lush pocket of land on the ocean has been labeled Punta Izopo National Park, and contrarily marked with one of the Private Property signs that are becoming more and more common in the area.

On a shack in the park is a banner advertising "Garifuna Tours."

"None of these tours you see advertised are run by the community," said Gregoria Flores, a resident of San Juan and president of OFRENAH, the Black Fraternal Organization of Honduras. "This one is run by Italians. These are outsiders coming in."

Bitter and bloody land struggles like the Garifuna are involved in are raging all over the country of Honduras, unbeknownst to most of the world. At the same time the Garifuna, Lenca, Miskito and other indigenous people are fighting for the right to remain on their traditional land, campesinos, many of whom are also indigenous, are struggling to establish or hold on to communities where they can plant enough food to feed their families and eke out a meager survival. ("Campesinos" is the term used to refer to people who are peasant farmers and identify primarily as such, whether or not they are indigenous. They consider themselves to have rights to the land because they are working on it, whereas indigenous groups claim ancestral rights to their native land regardless of how the land is being used.)

The country is full of landless peasants, many who end up fighting with each other or with indigenous groups for small areas of farmable land. For example, four tribes of indigenous Tulopane people who live in the high, remote Montaña de la Flor area say their land has been invaded by a group of campesinos, many of them also indigenous Tulopane, calling themselves "Los Invincibles." Cipriano Martinez, cacique (or leader) of one of the tribes, said they have been pleading with the government for at least two years to provide them basic health and education resources and emergency food aid, as well as police protection from Los Invincibles and other invaders.

"One of our biggest problems is invasion by people who

are settling in the land owned by the four tribes," said Martinez. "They are making it hard for us to live, work and raise our animals. We need a police post in the area and a doctor, but we are ignored. There was a missing person in the area and the body was found, but when we brought it to the authorities, they didn't want to even look into it."

Other campesino and indigenous leaders note that situations like that at Montaña de la Flor are complex and hard to negotiate, since there is an overall lack of land available for farming, while much land stands fallow, held but unused by the government or large landowners. Under agrarian reform laws, land that is not being used for "production" or "social purposes" can be legally reclaimed and redistributed by the National Agrarian Institute (INA). However, the government has been reluctant to carry out agrarian reform. The Modernization of the Agriculture Sector law passed in 1992 and other recent reforms have also watered down the original reform laws. So it is regular practice for campesinos and indigenous people to take matters into their own hands. Honduran peasants are actually among the most organized in Latin America, with a wide range of campesino organizations supporting groups of peasants in establishing communities complete with homes, farms and schools on unused "reclaimed" land.

Once they have occupied the land, the campesinos can file for legal title with INA and in many cases they are awarded the deeds. Things are never that simple, however, and often the original owner, be it an individual, government entity or corporation, will resurface demanding the land back. Evictions of the community will then be carried out, usually with the aid of police, often turning violent. At least 38 campesinos and indigenous people have been killed in land struggles since 1985.[52]

On March 28, 2002, four campesinos in the Empresa Campesina 1 de octubre organization were murdered by guards hired by Standard Fruit de Honduras, a subsidiary of U.S.-based Dole, as they walked along a trail to work in the Belfate municipality of the Colon province.[53] The 20 guards, armed with AK-47s, were lying in wait on land owned but largely unused by the U.S.-based company and occupied since October by the campesino community. In a brief statement issued to press, Standard Fruit said the deaths occurred in a mutual confrontation between armed peasants and the guards. Four guards were jailed for the killings, but were released a week later. COCOCH,[54] the national umbrella organization of campesino groups, has called for the government's human rights commission and the Supreme Court to investigate the killings. COCOCH also alleges that Standard Fruit is in violation of ILO Convention 107 for owning land within 40 kilometers of the coast.

Meanwhile, days after the 1 de octubre campesinos were killed, 220 women who in June 2001 established the country's largest community of all female-headed households on land owned by the National Autonomous University of Honduras in the Atlantida state were fearing a violent confrontation of their own. The women, mostly single mothers who work together to plant crops and care for and educate 350 children, were in the process of filing for legal title to the 69 hectares of land known as Jardin Clonal after the agricultural experiment the university was supposed to be carrying out there. The university never started the project, according to INA, and instead the land was being used for small dairy and other projects for the personal profit of local officials.

A March 13, 2002 letter from INA to Congress notes that the university was using only 14 manzanas (less than a hectare each) for a dairy and one for citrus. The letter said the land had been "deficiently managed" and "not fulfilling its purpose," leading INA to support the women's right to the land. "They need the land for agriculture, horticulture, aviculture and the construction of homes," the letter said.

But in early April 2002, INA was overruled by another governmental body, which decided in favor of the university. The university had filed criminal charges of usurpation against

48 members of the community, including minors, and there were four arrest warrants out. Women from the community said they have received numerous death threats and expect there to be violence if the eviction order is carried out.

"This is the first time women have led a struggle like this in Honduras," said Maria Alicia Calles, president of COCOCH. "This should be not just a local issue but an international issue. We need the solidarity of everyone, especially the percent of the population that are women."

On March 26, 2002, 111 families in the indigenous Lenca community of 20 de abril were evicted from beautiful mountain land in the La Paz province by over 100 police officers who removed the tin roofs from houses and burned them to the ground with all belongings inside. Community leaders think the eviction was ordered by the owner of the land, the widow of a wealthy Honduran businessman. They say his ownership violated land reform laws limiting the number of parcels that can be owned by one individual.

A week later, with the support of a militant campesino organization called the CNTC,[55] the 20 de abril community had reoccupied the land and begun rebuilding their homes.

"The landowners have so much power, they think they can do whatever they want," said Irene Hernandez, a CNTC official in the region. "We indigenous people are treated as if we have fewer rights than cows. In order to gain title to this land, we know it will be a struggle of years and we know we might lose the lives of some of our compañeros. But despite the obstacles we are committed to fight."

Meanwhile over 50 families in the La Sabana town in the Santa Barbara state had to live in tents made of tarp and sticks by the side of the highway after their two co-operatives, called Nuevo Despertar and Piñares del Lago, were leveled by bulldozers in March 2002. Nuevo Despertar and Piñares actually have titles to the land, which they had occupied for 14 and 29 years, but reportedly an NGO that professes to promote rural development and a government official also have legal titles preceding the campesinos' titles. Meanwhile, the campesinos say they are surviving thanks only to charity from groups in the nearby city of Santa Barbara.

"In the moments we were watching the machines tear down our homes, we felt totally alone, surrounded only by the enemy," said Herman Magdona Sosa, a leader of the Piñares community who has lived there with his family for 28 years. In his pocket he carries a painstakingly written list of all the families who have lost their homes. "What the government is doing is shameful, destroying our homes and putting our children out on the street."

"This NGO claims they want to promote the health, housing, education," said Jose Adolfo Sanchez, president of Nuevo Despertar. "But the opposite is true, because our campesinos are building developments and they are destroying them."

When the bulldozers came, community members including women and children were taken away in chains.

"By 11:30 am they were here picking up men, women, children, elders, anyone who was on the street and taking them to court in restraints, chained at the feet as if we were common criminals," said Sanchez.

This was also the experience of the 15 de mayo community in the mountains of La Paz, who have been evicted from their land four times, most recently in August 2001.

Each time they came back; during the last attempted eviction they prevented bulldozers from entering the village by blocking the highway with sticks and machetes. Twelve residents spent eight days in jail, but through organizing and lobbying by the CNTC they were able to hold on to the community. Today survival is still a daily struggle, with dire shortages of food and water and the nearest town hours away over a steep, pitted dirt road.

"People here are very strong," said Rosalio Murcia Portillo, former president of the CNTC. "We made a line across the highway with our machetes and sticks and stones, and we were able to stop the wave of repression, the bulldozers couldn't come in."

Indigenous and campesino leaders expect the land crunch to get even worse, with free trade agreements like the FTAA on the table.

On April 17, 2002, the international Day of the Campesino, thousands marched in the capital of Tegucigalpa demanding meaningful land reform and opposing free trade. President Ricardo Maduro publicly vowed to crack down on land reclamations and demonstrations such as the April 17 march, as part of his "zero tolerance" policy. But campesino and indigenous leaders say they are determined to keep up their struggle; they have no choice.

*As the Garifuna in San Juan Bautista waited for the police to arrive at the disputed lot they were occupying, they brought out traditional African drums and the electric tensions morphed into a scene of celebration and resistance as the men and women, boys and girls danced the traditional hip-gyrating "punta" and chanted in their native tongue under the shade of a lone tree. Eventually Gregoria Flores left with members of Pastors for Peace, a U.S.-based solidarity group visiting the community. Later in the day six police officers and a government attorney came to the site with an arrest warrant for Flores. At a press conference in Tegucigalpa the next day, Flores, a large woman with flowing dreadlocks and bright eyes, vowed to continue the fight for land, echoing the sentiment of the older women who stood in the sun in the lot, legs stolidly apart and faces set in placid determination.*

*"I'm 82 and I've never sold my land," said a small, wiry woman in a meeting that day in the San Juan community center, decorated with crepe paper and posters for the Miss Verano (Miss Summer) 2002 festivities. "And no one's going to take it from me."*

For more information:

Pastors for Peace, www.ifconews.org.

La Voz de los de Abajo: http://students.depaul.edu/~amaganal.

Luis Cardona (right) marches for justice for assassinated union-ist and fellow union member Isidro Segundo Gil in Bogota, Colombia.

# CHAPTER FIVE

# "Killer Coke"
## Global Refresher or Represser?

Q-tip, Q-tip," Karen Cardona croons as she caresses a black and white cat on the floor of a house in Little Village, a mostly Mexican neighborhood on Chicago's southwest side one afternoon in December 2003.

Cardona, nine, is outgoing and ebullient as she trots around the house, taking breaks from her homework to pet Q-tip and a Rottweiler mix named Iris.

Like her father Luis Adolfo Cardona, Karen loves animals. Luis had in fact wanted to be a veterinarian in their home country of Colombia, where his house was filled with dogs, cats, hamsters and other animals. He was also nearly a professional soccer player. But what he ended up doing was working at a Coca-Cola bottling plant in the town of Carepa.

And that job choice, ultimately, is what led Luis, Karen and Luis's wife Luzmary to Chicago, a continent away from their beloved home.

The Cardonas fled Colombia in fear for their lives because Luis, now 44, was a leader of the labor union at the bottling plant.

Cardona started working at the Carepa plant in 1984 after other workers recruited him to play on the company soccer team.

In 1986, workers organized with the SINALTRAINAL union to demand better wages, benefits and working conditions. The company owners and managers didn't like it one bit. So they employed members of one of the brutal, armed paramilitary groups which operate with almost total impunity in Colombia to do their dirty work. As the union was being organized, members of the United Self-Defense Forces of Colombia (UAC is the Spanish acronym), one of the country's most notorious paramilitary groups, began threatening union organizers. They would make phone calls to their houses and leave threatening notes under their doors.[56]

"Then they came directly to the leaders at the union hall and said if you don't leave, we will kill you," said Cardona. "That was happening at all the Coke plants in Colombia."

The bottling plants aren't owned by the Coca-Cola Co. itself but by other companies which contract with the Atlanta-based corporation. The Carepa plant is operated by the company Bebidas y Alimentos, which is owned by Richard Kirby of Key Biscayne, Fla.[57]

For decades union members all over Colombia have been subject to intimidation, terror and murder by paramilitary members working at the behest of company owners. The Colombian trade union federation CUT reports that 45 trade unionists were murdered in the first eight months of 2003, and 117 or more were murdered in 2002.[58]

On Dec. 5, 1996, paramilitaries came to the Carepa plant in the morning and assassinated union leader Isidro Segundo Gil, who as the union secretary was involved in ongoing negotiations for a better contract.

Ten shots were fired at Gil.

That same day, paramilitaries armed with pistols kidnapped Cardona, who was the secretary of recreation and sports for the union. "They took me outside the town, they said they were going to take me to a center where they torture and kill people," he said. "They said they were going to kill me. I was terrified."

Seven armed paramilitaries took him part of the way in a car, and as they were exiting the car to get on motorbikes Cardona saw his chance to escape.

"We had to cross the street, and as we were in the middle of the street I saw that I had to escape then or never," he said.

He was able to ditch the paramilitaries and ran to a nearby police station. Even though the police generally support the paramilitaries and grant them impunity, he noted, they couldn't allow the paramilitaries to take him in broad daylight, so for the time being he was safe.

"When I entered the police station words had left me, I was so afraid," he said. "I couldn't stop shaking."

He went home and got his wife and daughter and some important things, and headed to the union's national office in Bogota.

Meanwhile that same night the union's offices were set on fire, destroying their equipment and records. And the next day heavily armed paramilitaries came to the plant, gathered the workers together and told them if they didn't quit the union by 4 p.m. they'd be killed.

Cardona said the company would tell the workers that they had good pay and benefits, so they didn't need a union.

"But we had gotten all of that because of the union," he said. "If it wasn't for the union we would have the lowest pay, the worst benefits."

Fearing for their lives, about 60 of the about 100 workers at the plant quit and fled the area. The union was crushed, and new workers were hired at wages less than half what the union members had been making—about $130 a month compared to about $380.

Paramilitaries camped outside the plant for two months, and intimidation against the remaining workers continued. Three weeks after Gil's murder, Jose Librado Herrera Osorio was killed at the Carepa plant. He was at least the fifth Carepa worker to be killed between April 1994 and the end of 1996. Gil's wife was also killed later that year.[59]

Meanwhile Cardona spent nine months in Bogota. He was in a protection program for victims of violence, but the program lasted only six months and then he was on his own again. He tried living in other cities, but the paramilitaries would hunt him down. In 1999 he went back to Bogota, still constantly under threat of murder from the paramilitaries.

"They were going from town to town asking about me," he said. "They were trying to kill me."

He tried to get protection from the government and the union, but there were no adequate programs.

"The union gave me a bulletproof vest," he said, and a government ministry gave him a cell phone.

"But if someone's looking to kill you, what will a cell phone do?"

Then he found out about a program sponsored by the AFL-CIO in the U.S. to protect Colombian union members. The program brings union members to the U.S. temporarily to give them a respite from danger. Cardona applied for the program, he was accepted and in April 2002 he arrived in Chicago.

After he came to Chicago Cardona's family remained in Colombia, but he was worried about their safety.

The separation was also painful for them. He said that when he talked to Karen on the phone she would put on a brave voice, but in reality she was losing a lot of weight, missing him and worrying about him horribly.

"She couldn't take baths alone because whenever she would look in the water she would see my face," he said.

When he called his home once and someone else answered but didn't say anything, he realized they were in serious danger. The United Steel Workers of America helped him do the paperwork to obtain tourist visas for his wife and daughter, who arrived in Chicago in the fall of 2002. With the AFL-CIO program coming to an end, the family applied for political asylum. The applications were approved, making them permanent legal residents of the U.S.

Now Cardona spends virtually all of his time attending rallies and giving talks about paramilitary violence in Colombia, and more generally about the effects of free trade and globalization in Latin America.

So far, he says, Coca-Cola has given him no answers or even apologies.

A letter written "on behalf" of Coca-Cola chairman and CEO Douglas Daft to the public said there was "no evidence" to support "outrageous allegations against the company and its bottling partners."[60]

But Cardona says Coke could hold its bottlers accountable if they really wanted to.

"Coke says they have nothing to do with [events in] Colombia, that these are about social problems," said Cardona. "But it's their responsibility. And the owners of the plants are North Americans. They don't want unions because they'll have to pay higher salaries, so they don't speak out against violence against unionists."

In July 2001 at the behest of SINALTRAINAL, the United Steel Workers of America and International Labor Rights Fund filed a lawsuit in U.S. District Court in the Southern District of Florida under the Alien Tort Claim Act, charging Coca-Cola, its largest Latin American bottler, the Panamerican Beverage Co. (Panamco) and their subsidiaries with allowing kidnapping, torture and intimidation to be visited upon union activists.[61] The suit, which seeks $500 million in damages, is still in litigation.

Panamco's 2002 annual report responds that, "The Company believes this lawsuit is without merit and intends to vigorously defend itself in this matter."[62]

While Colombia is infamous for political murders and violence, attacks on workers at Coca-Cola bottling plants have occurred in other countries as well.

Eight union members at a Coke bottling plant in Guatemala City were killed between 1975 and 1980—it took a year-long factory occupation and an international solidarity campaign and boycott to finally get a collective bargaining agreement for that plant in 1985.[63]

Henry Frundt, a New Jersey sociology professor who wrote

a book about Coca-Cola in Guatemala called "Refreshing Pauses," noted that at one point the bottling plant was owned by Texan John Trotter.

"He was a very conservative guy, with ties to the Guatemala military, who arranged for workers to be intimidated, harassed and eventually killed," said Frundt in an interview. "The stories of what they did are like a spy novel. The head of Coke in Mexico at the time would visit the plant wearing a wig and dark glasses because he was so afraid. He told me he knew there were problems there but he didn't want to get involved."

Frundt said the international campaign forced Trotter to sell the plant in 1980, to a Mexican owner who had better labor practices but "ended up basically bankrupting it, " leading to more labor problems and the year-long occupation by workers in 1984.

When workers at Pepsi's Mariposa plant in Guatemala attempted to unionize in 1993, management released memos blaming the attempt on Coca-Cola workers' example. Reports from workers said that salesmen were being ordered to steal and destroy at least 150 cases of Coca-Cola a day, likely with the intention of encouraging confrontations between Coke and Pepsi workers and weakening solidarity.

In 2003 Panamco was bought by Coca-Cola FEMSA, a conglomerate of the Coca-Cola Co. and the Mexican company FEMSA.[64] Up until then Panamco had operated as an "anchor bottler" franchise of Coca-Cola, manufacturing, selling and distributing soft drinks with Coca-Cola supplying the concentrate.[65]

A 1998 report from an international union called IUF[66] explains Coke's relationship with Panamco and other 'anchor bottlers,' which makes it clear that—contrary to its claims—Coke has plenty of control over these companies.

"The Coca-Cola Company retains total control of its concentrate, as well as of all major strategic and marketing decisions. Together with its substantial minority ownership share (usually 30 to 49 percent) in the anchor bottler, this ensures that Coca-Cola remains the controlling partner in the business relationship. Coca-Cola calls this process 'alignment.' The bottlers support Coke's expansion plans, swap strategies and even executives."[67]

Thus as with the maquilas where workers toil in unsafe conditions with little oversight or legal protection, the U.S.-based Coca-Cola Co. is able to make significant profits off its Latin American operations without being held accountable for the conditions at its bottling plants. The situation with Coca-Cola is an especially stirring symbol of corporate globalization and its effects, since the beverage is so pervasive in Latin America and is marketed as and seen as the epitome of the U.S. and the "good life."

In Ecuador, for example, Christmas time finds the country awash in nativity scenes and sparkling lights. But even more than traditional and Catholic Christmas decorations, Christmas in Ecuador means Coca-Cola.

El Malecón 2000, the modern "millennium park" in the city of Guayaquil, sports a huge Christmas tree covered in over-size Coke bottle caps, next to a larger than life diorama of the famous Coca-Cola polar bear. Nearby a full size model cabin shows a homey scene complete with Coca-Cola curtains in the windows, posters of Coca-Cola on the walls and of course bottles of Coke on the table and in the refrigerator. In upscale malls in the city, the department store Santas are decked out in Coca-Cola regalia.

Sentimental Coke T.V. ads showing people in remote areas all over the world happily guzzling the sweet brown beverage are not far from the truth—from the remote jungle areas of Chiapas, Mexico to the Andean slopes of Ecuador; from the tiny thatch-roofed roadside towns of Bolivia and Peru to the sparkling major metropolises of Chile and Argentina, Coke is all over Latin America. Not only the beverage itself, but an infinite number of ads that blanket everything from billboards to

Coke is as ubiquitous as images of revolutionary Che Guevara
throughout Latin America. Photo by Kari Lydersen.

shacks to government buildings to the concrete walls along mountain roadways.

Coke was introduced to Latin America four decades after it was first invented by pharmacist John Pemberton in Atlanta in 1886. By 1927 it was being sold in Honduras, Colombia and Mexico, along with Haiti and Burma. The next year it debuted in Venezuela, and in 1942 Nicaragua, Argentina, Brazil, Costa Rica and Uruguay got in on the action. Today Mexico has one of the world's highest per capita consumption levels of Coke, along with Iceland, and Bolivia has the distinction of the world's highest bottling plant at 12,000 feet.[68]

A 1998 report by Panamco said the average Latin American drinks 312 servings of Coca-Cola beverages a year (including other brands of soda produced by the company, but traditional Coca-Cola is the most popular).[69]

These levels weren't reached by accident. Panamco's marketing strategies are rich in military-esque terminology with the clear intent of complete domination.

A 1998 Panamco report describes how in Costa Rica, it "rolled out the 100 Meters Program and Red Blast project in several regions, developing new nontraditional channels in areas of high pedestrian traffic to stimulate impulse consumption." The 100 Meters Program, also implemented in parts of Mexico, aimed to "advocate availability of cold product within 100 meters of all consumers."[70]

It notes that the campaign included the widespread distribution of the "metallic posters, flags and neon signs" that pepper Latin America like a rash "to call attention to our products, [and] instill a perception of value in the consumer."

In Costa Rica the company also initiated a "School" plan aimed at increasing the presence of Coke in schools.

And in Nicaragua, in 1998 Panamco launched a "Roots" plan that "aimed to transform small, traditional outlets into 'red' outlets by equipping clients with tailored merchandising materials, installing coolers and painting establishments in

Coca-Cola colors." This program resulted in a 40 percent boost in client sales, according to the report, homogenizing tiny local businesses but "generating client satisfaction and loyalty."

Panamco's 2002 annual report notes that net revenue was down 10 percent from the previous year, partly due to currency devaluations in Venezuela, Mexico and Brazil. But the company still managed to take in $2.4 billion in net revenue.[71]

The man who is ushering in the FTAA, Plan Puebla-Panama and other free trade projects in Mexico, President Vicente Fox, actually honed his political and business skills as an executive at Coca-Cola de Mexico, where he worked for 15 years. Leading up to and during the 2000 election he was often referred to as "the Coca-Cola kid."

This is appropriate since in Mexico, as in the rest of Latin America, homages to the beverage and what it symoblizes are everywhere. In a shantytown in Tijuana, housing impoverished maquila workers who have migrated to the border from other parts of Mexico, one of the shacks is constructed partly out of a discarded banner advertising Coke. The slogan on the dusty canvas says it all.

"Disfrutala"…"Enjoy It."

For more information:

U.S. Labor Education in the Americas Project: www.usleap.org

Colombia Report: www.colombiareport.org

Colombia Action Network: www.colombiaactionnet-work.org

www.stopkillercoke.org.

A woman ekes out a living recycling bottles in El Alto, Bolivia.
Photo by Kari Lydersen.

# CHAPTER SIX

# Teatro Trono
## Bolivians Act Out

The market in a dusty neighborhood of El Alto, Bolivia is bustling. The snow-capped peaks of the Andes tower above the low-slung brick buildings of this city located on a plateau just above the capitol of La Paz, at an altitude of about 12,000 feet. Stocky indigenous women with thick black braids, voluminous pleated skirts and colorful shawls holding babies or bags of food on their backs preside over stalls selling nuts, green bars of soap, spiral notebooks and countless other products. Teenagers in western clothes meander down the street and children in woolen hats run shrieking playfully between stalls.

Suddenly, the sound of pounding drumbeats permeates the air, causing the bins of peanuts and dried peppers and grains to vibrate. Toward one end of the market three young men dressed in colorful, carnival-esque costumes dance wildly. A crowd gathers around them, taking in the throbbing, primal energy of the drums and dance. Then a woman in black announces that this is Teatro Trono, here to offer a completely free theater performance. The dancers and drummers, young men wearing masks, one in a black velvet vest with gold braid and mirrors on it, start gyrating toward the nearby Plaza Miner, leading the entranced crowd behind them Pied Piper-style.

The theater performance starts under the watchful eyes of the life-size statues at the center of the plaza—two miners in yellow suits and helmets, looks of steely determination in their eyes. El Alto is home to many miners, traditionally one of the country's most militant and powerful workforces until the industry virtually disappeared over the past few decades. Teatro Trono starts with a circus performance—two young men in face paint and shiny clothes ride in circles on unicycles, and kids cavort around tossing and twirling brightly colored rings, pins and balls. A few times the crowd scatters to avoid flying disks that have been tossed too high. The men, women and children laugh and stare, mesmerized by the demonstration.

Gustavo Analoca, 27, one of the unicycle riders, takes the stage for a solo performance, doing a series of tricks with a disk balanced on string between two sticks. Analoca was one of the founders of Teatro Trono, which was started by a man named Ivan Nogales at a rehabilitation and detention center for boys in La Paz in 1989. Analoca, 13 at the time, ended up there after escaping from an orphanage where he had lived for eight years after his parents split up and were no longer able to care for him. Analoca is now the circus instructor for Teatro Trono, and dreams of opening his own circus school for street kids in El Alto.

After the circus performance, Teatro Trono members do a series of skits. The Tronitos, the youngest actors, become animals and celestial bodies for skits titled "The Hunter" and "The Caprices of the Sun and Moon." Teenage girls do one of the group's trademark pieces, which they have performed often during their multiple NGO-funded trips to Europe and Chicago. The piece is called "The International Market," developed from an old radio play. In the skit indigenous people discover the joys of cacao and how to make it into chocolate. Then an English-speaking trader in a cardboard ship comes, smells the chocolate and offers to buy the cacao from them at one peso per pound. Then she returns to sell the chocolate back to them at 10 pesos a pound. The indigenous people decide to start their own chocolate-making operation and sell it for five pesos per pound, but the trader undercuts them with prices of two pesos per pound and even hires them to work in her factory, loading them on the boat to another land.

"This is the way it happens in the international market," says the one dissident who wouldn't go work in the factory. "It's always the same."

"This was written 30 years ago, but it's even more relevant today," noted Coral Salazar Gonzalez, 26, a slender woman with big eyes and long black hair who along with her sister Ana is a theater instructor at Teatro Trono.

Indeed the effects of the international market and globalization are visible and tangible everywhere in El Alto, La Paz and Bolivia as a whole. Many Bolivian academics and social leaders describe it as a country without a developed economy or market of its own, thrust too quickly into the global, free trade market and suffering as a result. The day of Teatro Trono's performance, March 6, 2004, is Dia del Alto, the anniversary of the city. But this year it isn't being celebrated as usual, out of respect for the over 40 deaths that occurred here in October 2003 during the "Gas War" that ousted President Gonzalo Sánchez de Lozada.

Marco Bazan, a staff member at Teatro Trono, takes a break from feeding salami sandwiches to the hungry young actors to describe the uprising. Building up during a year of various labor struggles, protests and roadblocks by indigenous people, campesinos, workers and students throughout the country, the Gas War started in earnest in September 2003 with a series of roadblocks protesting the government's IMF-backed plan to sell natural gas to the U.S. through Chile. Besides a long-standing animosity with Chile over territory disputes, the plan was seen as the latest attempt to launch the country into the global market at the expense of the majority of the population. Rather than selling off natural resources to pay external debt and appease the IMF, people argued, the government should be developing and reinvesting in domestic industries. The gas plan "doesn't resolve the structural problem of Bolivia, the need for genuine resources for development," notes the newsletter of a La Paz labor center.[72] Along with protesting the gas plan, people were also demanding better wages and social services, the release of political prisoners, an end to the systematic eradication of coca (the only viable economic alternative for many farmers), and the rejection of the FTAA.

The September roadblocks prevented the transport of goods and stranded about 1,000 tourists, many of them U.S. citizens, in the town of Sorata. The military initiated an armed stand-off with indigenous people in Sorata and Warisata that left six dead, including one soldier. In early October the conflict spread to El Alto, where miners and indigenous people blocked roads and access to the Senkata diesel plant. The military descended with tear gas, firearms and helicopters, trying to clear the way for trucks with cisterns to remove diesel from the plant. Between Oct. 9 and Oct. 12 at least 37 people were killed.[73]

"The economic struggles, or the 'Gas Wars,' were converted into a race war," says a recent book about indigenous uprisings, called "Ya Es Otro Tiempo El Presente." The book notes that anyone who "resisted a mestizo official was killed without pity."[74]

"At first the protests were peaceful," said Bazan, a man in his mid-30s with a warm smile and a short, braided "rat- tail" hairstyle. "But the government said they would get the diesel no matter what. That's when the killings happened, when they were bringing cisterns in to take the diesel."

In the ensuing days, 100,000 people from El Alto descended into La Paz, with cries of "El Alto on foot, not on its knees," and "Civil War!"

"Every day we would march down to La Paz," said Bazan, down the breathtakingly steep and rugged cliffs that separate El Alto from the capitol.

"All kinds of people, old women, men, kids," he said. "People like me who aren't political. If it hadn't been for the deaths, this wouldn't have happened. But we couldn't stand to see innocent people massacred like that. We marched down to La Paz from all sides, every day. We weren't afraid. We felt it in our hearts."

The uprising quickly spread to La Paz and the rest of the country. Indigenous Quechuas and Aymaras, cocaleros (coca farmers), students, displaced miners and campesinos, even some middle-class professionals joined the protests, strikes and blockades that paralyzed the country. When Sánchez de Lozada, unaffectionately known as "Goni," resigned and fled the country and vice president Carlos de Mesa took over on Oct. 17, 70 or more had been killed and many more injured. The majority of the deaths occurred in El Alto.

Coral Salazar and Gustavo Analoca were scheduled to leave for a European tour with 10 Teatro Trono youth when the uprising broke out. "All the roads were closed, there was broken glass everywhere," Salazar said. "A lot of flights were cancelled. We had to walk miles with all our luggage to the military airport, which never closes. You had to cover your face to breathe because of all the tear gas. It was hard, but all our friends and all the kids' relatives came out to help us."

Like most Latin American countries, Bolivia is clearly divided into a small mostly white or mestizo wealthy class and a vast impoverished population, with the chasm between them growing wider every day. On a sunny afternoon in late February 2004, just after the celebrations of Carnaval have swept the city, these divisions are crystallized in the Plaza Eduardo Abaroa in a well-off, tree-lined neighborhood of downtown La Paz. A poodle in a red sweater catapults over low walls playfully chasing a delighted little boy in camouflage pants. A fashionably slender, light-skinned girl in pre-faded bell bottom jeans of the type popular in the U.S. strolls by holding a tiny puppy. Kids career around in small motorized cars; a little girl bawls as her father lifts her off the car to give her sister a chance. But parallel to this scene of perfect leisure and enjoyment are plenty of examples of people struggling just to make a living. Indigenous women with their babies on their backs sell salteñas (chicken-filled pockets of dough) and trinkets.

Little boys and young men dressed in dark clothes with ski masks or rags covering their faces, giving them a menacing look, troll the plaza with wooden shoe shine kits. Some just point at people's feet before being waved away or granted a shoe shine. One 13-year-old boy, his face uncovered and a mildly stoned

A young Teatro Trono member drums in Plaza Miner in El Alto, Bolivia on the anniversary of the "gas war." Photo by Kari Lydersen.

look in his eyes, oozes an uncomfortable flirtatiousness as he asks me to give him a kiss and buy him an icecream or soft drink. When I ask to interview him for the price of a shoe shine (one boliviano, or about 15 cents in the U.S.), he no longer seems seedy or stoned but becomes immediately serious. His name is Luis Gabriel Quispe Guzman. "People are poor, there's no work here," he says. He's been shining shoes since he was six years old, and he makes about 15 bolivianos, less than $2 U.S., each day.

Cousins Christian, 8, and Enrique, 10, are also shoeshine boys. They sit protectively next to each other across the street from the plaza on the steps of a café serving mostly wealthy Bolivians and tourists. Next door is a plastic surgeon's office. Leaning against a wall nearby is an older shoe-shiner, his face completely covered with gray material with only two eye-holes cut out. Christian and Enrique have worked as shoe shine boys on weekends since their families moved to El Alto four years ago from the country town of Warisata, one of the cradles of the Gas War. They go to school during the week. Enrique wants to be a lawyer, "to defend our people, because we don't have anyone to defend us." Christian says he wants to be a police officer, but when Enrique tells him that the police are bad he changes his mind to being a professional soccer player. Christian and Enrique have bright eyes and friendly open faces, theirs uncovered. Little Christian seems to have a chronically runny nose above his gap-toothed smile. When an even tinier boy, a 6-year-old, sits down beside them and pipes up that he too is from El Alto, Christian rounds us up to talk somewhere else and warns that the boy will try to steal my coffee.

"He's very badly behaved," he says. "His brother is a ratero," meaning a thief or hustler.

Like the majority of people in the country, the boys' whole families are employed in the informal economy. Christian's father washes cars and his brother also shines shoes. Enrique's mother sells vegetables and his father "is in the cemetery being eaten by ants."

When asked why the shoe shine boys cover their faces, the boys give an answer that contradicts the sinister look the masks give them. "Because they're ashamed," says Enrique, noting that Christian often covers his face. "They don't want their professors from school to see them."

Claudio Urey Miranda, one of the founding members of Teatro Trono and a street kid for many years, confirms this explanation. "It's a denigrating job," says Urey, 30, who now works at a residential center for drug and alcohol addicted people in the tropical city of Santa Cruz about a 20-hour bus ride from La Paz. "A lot of them are in school. They have to shine shoes to make money, but if there's a girl they like they don't want her to see them all dirty."

Alvaro Garcia Linera, a sociology professor at the Mayor San Andres University, says that 68 percent of Bolivia's population are employed in the informal economy. That's up from 50 percent in 1980, he noted during an interview in his downtown apartment, lined with tomes by Marx, Engels and Gramsci. Frequently brushing his stylishly cut hair out of his eyes, Garcia rattles off other statistics showing how life has gotten harder for average Bolivians as the country has tried to leap into the global economy. He notes that official unemployment, usually considered to be vastly under-reported, has tripled to 12 percent today from four percent in 1980. Unofficial church figures put the number at closer to 40 percent. He says the average wage in 1980 was $950 U.S. a year; today it is $830.

"The process of globalization and integration (into the world market) have really hit the local traditional economies hard," he said. "Especially the labor sectors with little competitive capacity and archaic technology. We were thrown into the open market before we'd developed the competitiveness for it."

He noted that a huge percent of the population, particularly indigenous people, have long survived through traditional micro-economies based on small-scale agriculture and craftsmanship and the free use of natural resources. But now their agricultural and other products can't compete in the market, and even their natural resources are being privatized by foreign companies.

"3.8 million campesinos live through traditional family and community economies," Garcia said. "But now they're being struck by foreign investment and privatization. The Water War is an example of that."

Like the Gas War, the Water War, or La Guerra del Agua, is spoken of almost reverently all over the country. Cochabamba, Bolivia's third largest city, is located between the jungle area known as the Chapare and the high barren Altiplano, not far from the country's prime coca-growing regions. On a lovely evening in March 2004, the city's palm-lined plaza fills with residents coming to hear a brass band, couples making out on benches, black-clad teenagers waiting for a concert by the rock band Mago de Oz (Wizard of Oz) the following night.

Exactly four years ago, in the late winter and spring of 2000, this plaza and the surrounding streets were ground zero of the Water War, where the people of Cochabamba squared off against a multinational company with annual revenue over five times as large as the government of Bolivia's entire budget.

In September 1999, after years of pressure and negotiations by the World Bank and International Monetary Fund, the Bolivian government signed a 40-year contract with the conglomerate Aguas del Tunari (AdT) making it the sole provider of water and sanitation services to the city of about one million. AdT is a conglomerate of foreign companies, with the largest interest-holder being the U.S. construction company Bechtel,[75] known for its controversial contracts for the rebuilding of Iraq, among other things.

Going along with the contract, in October 1999 the government passed the Drinking and Sanitation Law, law 2029, allowing for the privatization of drinking water and sewage services. Within weeks of taking over Cochabamba´s water system, Bechtel raised prices about 200 percent, with the justification that it had improved service and was charging equivalent rates per services offered to what people had paid before. In a way this was true; before the takeover most of the city relied on local sometimes haphazard community water networks that in many areas only provided water during certain parts of the day or week. But the rates Bechtel charged for its "improved" service amounted to 25 percent or more of a family´s wages for residents of the poorer parts of the city, so many families were left with no water at all. Water bills published in a local paper showed an increase from 113 to 259 bolivarianos for the same amount of usage over a matter of days in January 2000.

And AdT´s contract also included a guaranteed 16 percent return on its investments,[76] a lucrative deal considering that in the U.S. water companies earned 6 to 12.5 percent average profits in 1991, when profits for French and English companies were around 6 percent.[77]

The company refused to respond to the demands of the public and local community and social justice groups to reduce their water rates or subsidize poorer families. So starting in January 2000, tens of thousands of people took to the streets in Cochabamba demanding Bechtel´s contract be terminated and that water be made affordable for all. In January the city was shut down for four days with road blocks and a general strike in protest over the water rates. In February three months of protest and blockades started, shutting down the city for weeks at a time. The initial peaceful protests turned violent after police responded with tear gas and brutality.

The resistance was coordinated largely by a group called the Coordinadora Departmental de la Defensa del Agua (the Coordinadora). The movement is widely described as a democratic, grassroots effort with a variety of local leaders; the most public faces were those of Evo Morales, a popular leader of cocaleros (coca farmers) who nearly won the presidency in 2002 and Oscar Olivera, an anti-globalization activist and member of the Coordinadora.

In March 2000 the Coordinadora held a referendum on the water contract, with 50,000 voting and over 90 percent saying that the increased water tariffs should be annulled, that Bechtel's contract should be ended and that the country's Water Law which allowed the privatization should be scrapped.[78]

The government and AdT and Bechtel executives refused to listen, however, and the water war raged on. The city was completely shut down and the police attacked protesters with 12 kinds of gas and severe brutality. Olivera and other leaders were arrested during an April 6 meeting with government officials, which Olivera called a trap, and held in remote detention centers until they were released under massive pressure. A 17-year-old boy, Victor Hugo Daza, was killed by a military sniper firing into a crowd; the sniper was later acquitted of any charges. A local newspaper headline described the police who had been protecting an AdT billboard fleeing in fear as the public destroyed the sign. Protests and roadblocks spread to La Paz and all over the country, with people demanding the downfall of then-president Hugo Banzer and Bechtel. On April 8, 2000 Banzer declared a state of emergency in the country, allowing the suspension of constitutional rights and the detention of dissidents.

Then on April 10, the government signed an agreement with Olivera terminating the contract of AdT/Bechtel, promising to repeal the privatization law, releasing detained protesters and turning the control of water over to the Coordinadora.

The people were victorious, after the clashes that left at least four dead, up to 100 injured, and U.S. $110 million in damage to the city. "Schools, businesses, everything was closed," said Raul Salvatierra, a member of the Coordinadora. "There weren't even bikes in the streets. There were protests and blockades in every province. Bechtel was surprised to be frustrated in their ambitions to make all this money off our water."

The victory was celebrated a week later during international protests against globalization during the IMF's meeting in Washington D.C. There Olivera hailed the outcome of the water war, saying "people have recaptured their dignity, their capacity to organize themselves, and most importantly people are no longer scared."

Water privatization has been a major part of global policies instituted by the IMF and World Bank; today 460 million people around the world, compared to 51 million in 1990, depend on private water companies largely because of policies pushed by the World Bank and IMF.[79] While private companies often can improve the quality of water service, the profit motive that privatization brings into the equation means many people are also left, literally, out to dry.

After its contract was terminated Bechtel sued the country of Bolivia for $25 million in lost profits through a bilateral trade agreement with the Netherlands, where one of its subsidiaries is based. The lawsuit is still being heard in a secret tribunal of the World Bank's International Centre for the Settlement of Investment Disputes. The tribunal hearing the case consists of three representatives appointed by the World Bank, the Bolivian government, and AdT itself.[80] "Now Bechtel wants to settle, but we don't want to pay a cent to them," said Salvatierra, sitting in the Coordinadora's office in a ramshackle office building just off the main plaza, its walls lined with colorful posters decrying globalization and glorifying popular struggle. "They know what they're asking for isn't just."

A coalition of international groups including the Coordinadora and the U.S.-based Earthjustice filed a friend of the court brief asking the tribunal's proceedings be open to the public, but their request was denied.

Elizabeth Peredo, a social psychologist who works with the Fundacion Solon, an anti-gobalization NGO, noted that the $25 million Bechtel wants could pay 3,000 teachers to work in Bolivia's countryside for a year.

"For Bechtel, $25 million is their office expenses for a month," she said. Bechtel made over $14 billion in revenue in 2000, while Bolivia´s national budget at the same time was $2.7 billion.[81]

Given this disparity Peredo sees the lawsuit and the attempted privatization that preceded it as not only an economic disaster but a human rights violation. "It is a human rights violation, and it hurts the poor most, the indigenous most, and indigenous women the most of all," she said.

Peredo noted that not only did the privatization affect people´s health and daily lives, but their very philosophy of life. Water is central to everything from indigenous religious ceremonies to the more modern celebration of carnaval, which features water fights with squirt guns, water balloons and hoses for weeks all over Bolivia. A publication by Fundacion Solon says that, "Water comes from Wirakocha, the god who created the universe, who created Pachamama (Mother Earth) and permitted the reproduction of life. So divinity is present in the lakes, the lagoons, the sea, the rivers, all sources of water."[82]

"For years in Bolivia we´ve viewed water as a communal resource, indigenous people are used to collecting water and using water as a ritual, a way of community," Peredo said. "Bechtel not only raised the tariffs but attacked their whole vision of water and community."

Bechtel´s lawsuit mirrors the kind of lawsuits that could be commonplace if the proposed FTAA is passed; already similar lawsuits are allowed under Chapter 11 of NAFTA.

Meanwhile though the Water War was won, the battle for public ownership of water in Cochabamba and the rest of Bolivia is far from over. In Cochabamba, the Coordinadora and other organizations are working to develop a democratic, functioning form of water distribution that guarantees water to all and relies on democratic and inclusive decision-making procedures. Salvatierra, director of water distribution to the Zona Sur part of the city under this new system, notes that the majority of households in the area still rely on their own independent water systems. One of their major challenges now is incorporating them all into a centralized but democratic system.

"All the community members know us, so they will play a role in protecting the water networks and preventing the pirating of water," he said.

Under the new system households aren´t actually charged for water, only for the cost of transporting it, the necessary upgrading of infrastructure  and the administration of the system. A study is currently underway to determine exactly what those costs are. He notes that there will be a baseline cost for offering service, but many poor families won´t even be able to afford this cost.

"So we will use organic collective decision-making procedures to find out how to get water to those families," he said. "That´s the way we will address problems."

Though the community system may not be able to offer water 24 hours a day to everyone, and it will take a while to revamp the decrepit infrastructure, the vast majority of Cochabambinos still prefer it to Bechtel.

"We organized to recoup our human dignity, to not have to depend on some authority for our water," said Salvatierra. "Even if we can't improve the service we can say this is ours."

Though he said it is too early to say the new system has been a success, Salvatierra and others hope it can serve as a model for other communities around the world.

One of the reasons Cochabamba was ground zero for the water war was that it is extremely dry and difficult to obtain water.

Professor Garcia noted that even though the local water distribution in Cochabamba has been collectivized, they still must rely partly on private companies to get water to the city in the first place, piping it in from other places.

"It´s not their fault that there´s just not much water in Cochabamba," he said. "They´ve improved the service a little,

not a lot. They have a transparent process now, free from corruption. And they have stable tariffs. Those are small successes,
but to people who are used to things never getting better, that's
a big deal."

In La Paz, Bolivia's largest city at about 12,000 feet high,
water is more plentiful thanks to melting snow from the surrounding mountain ranges. But privatization is still an issue
here. The company Aguas del Illimani controls most of the
city's potable water, and there are moves under way to further
privatize the municipal water system.

Pablo Solon, director of Fundacion Solon, said the foundation and other groups are currently trying to change the
country's water laws, to among other things prohibit the export
of water. The government is planning to export water to northern Chile, where water is needed for the mining industry. They
have managed to have a law introduced in the national legisla-
ture which would prohibit water exportation.

"There's no water in northern Chile, so they want to take
it from us," he said.

The country's water laws were modified in response to the
water war, among other things to force companies like Aguas
del Illimani to charge their tariffs in the local bolivianos currency rather than dollars. But he said Aguas del Illimani and
other companies are resisting even this modification.

"We're pushing for the reform of the laws and the complete enforcement of the laws as they are (paying tariffs in bolivianos)," he said. "It's not just Aguas del Illimani we're fighting, it's also the World Bank. They don't want to change the
laws. They want laws favorable to international corporations."

In August 2003 in San Salvador, El Salvador people from
Cochabamba participated in an international conference on
fighting the privatization of water, where a declaration was
drawn up calling for the protection of water as a human right;
the exclusion of water privatization from FTAA and other free
trade treaties; the protection of the rights of indigenous people

as they relate to water; and other measures. The declaration proclaims that popular movements and organization are the only way to fight water privatization and exploitation at its root.[83]

A report from the conference notes that Latin America is home to 26 percent of the world's water resources, yet there are no laws protecting guaranteed access to water for everyone.

Peredo hopes the water war in Cochabamba will serve as an example and inspiration for other ongoing struggles against privatization. "This started out as a local issue in a country no one ever thinks about, but it turned into a fight with world-wide significance," she said.

Meanwhile it looks like the Water War and the Gas War are only the start. Things have been relatively calm in the four months since Sánchez de Lozada departed and Mesa took over. But many Bolivians describe this as the calm before the storm. Little has improved for the masses of Bolivians, and frustrations and internal divisions are festering. When asked what the coming months or years hold, many mention the possibility of civil war.

"There are three things that could happen," said Garcia, drawing a rainbow-shaped graphic to show the possibilities. "We could go back to the old regime, through a violent coupe, and it would become an authoritarian regime enforced by violence. Or we could have moderate reforms driven by the people. Or we could have a revolution led by left wing forces like Evo Morales and (indigenous leader) Felipe Quispe."

He places President Mesa right in the center of the left to right rainbow, and says that's the road the country is on now. But it could go either way; he sees things heading toward a big "fracaso," a big mess. That's largely because there are so many different and competing interests in the country, interests who were largely united during the October 2003 protests but ultimately have different leaders and different aims.

"Social movements are a powerful part of democracy," Garcia said. "Usually you have a social movement hitting the old regime, then you have a period of transition, then you have the new regime. We're in the period of transition now, and we hope we're heading toward a new regime. But we're fragmented, so we're in crisis."

Feliz Salazar Gonzalez, the father of Teatro Trono members Coral and Ana and a pedagogical student and author, sees the deep divisions in the country as the primary challenge and threat Bolivia faces.

"We aren't one nation, we're many nations, we speak 200 languages," said Salazar, 55, while playing with his grandson in his airy apartment in Santa Cruz. Salazar has published several novels about homeless youth, organized crime and corruption in the country, including one called "Yocazador" about an indigenous boy displaced to the city but dreaming of the native lands he has never seen.

"The situation now is worse than ever and I don't think it's going to improve," he said. "We're divided and the foreign economic interests exploit our divisions to increase their power."

As in many Latin American countries, one of the effects of economic distress and dislocation caused by privatization and globalization has been migration within and out of the country. Thousands of campesinos and indigenous people are leaving their homelands to try to survive in the cities, as difficult as that is. El Alto is made up largely of former miners, campesinos and indigenous people displaced from their homes. This migration is leading to the loss of indigenous language and culture, as indigenous youth who move to the cities "feel ashamed of their origin, imitate Western culture, form gangs imitating the style in T.V. shows, dance to rock music in discos and seldom or never participate in indigenous festivals," says "Ya Es Otro Tiempo El Presente."[84]

"There have been big social consequences from globalization," said Peredo. "People are going to the cities looking for work, even though there's almost no work there. People will live by selling lemons, even though they might only sell four lemons a day for 10 bolivianos (about $1.30 U.S.). Barely enough to buy food. But they'll be out there the next day selling lemons."

Finding they can't make a living in the city, thousands of Bolivians per year are also immigrating out of the country, mainly to Argentina and the U.S. The large population of Bolivians in Argentina face xenophobia, labor exploitation and discrimination, while those who travel the thousands of miles and pay the thousands of dollars to enter the U.S. illegally find the typical challenges of undocumented workers: low-paying and insecure jobs, the constant threat of deportation and separation from family. There are about 500,000 Bolivians in the U.S., with the majority of them living in the Arlington, Va. and Washington D.C. area as well as Los Angeles, Chicago and New York.[85] The Bolivian population in the U.S. is known as a hidden and humble population, without the visibility or growing political pull of the Mexican immigrant community, "more interested in avoiding notice than succeeding in getting any kind of power."[86]

The majority of Bolivian immigrants in the U.S. are campesinos who forever dream of returning to Bolivia but often never do. As in other Latin American countries, immigration has changed the nature of rural Bolivian life. "Because of immigration to the U.S. and Argentina, whole towns are practically depopulated," notes a United Nations report, and many couples spend "20 years, or 80 percent of their married life, apart."[87]

"Women are being forced to do what used to be considered men's work, because the men are all gone," said Peredo, whose work at Fundacion Solon includes a focus on women's rights.

Peredo notes that one of the things that HASN'T happened as a result of globalization and the weakening economy, however, is a major crime wave of the type taking place in other countries.

"People don't turn to delinquency here, you don't have to be afraid to walk in the street like in Colombia or Peru," she noted. "Even in this globalized culture where people want comfort and all the material things, we maintain our humanity and moral values. This is a form of resistance against globalization."

For Teatro Trono founder Ivan Nogales, fostering creativity and personal and collective growth is a major form of resistance. Teatro Trono grew out of the workshops that Nogales started doing in the boys detention and rehabilitation center in La Paz in 1989.

"Ivan was doing therapy with the kids, but it was much more than therapy," said Claudio Urey Miranda, who left his country town and ended up on the streets of La Paz after his parents both died when he was a teenager. His brother Angel, two years younger, was also at the detention center and joined the theater group. The boys lobbied to be able to leave the center to perform in different neighborhoods.

"They were afraid we would escape"—as Claudio had before, he noted. "No one could believe street kids could actually do something like this. But eventually they let us go, and we were on our best behavior. It was a huge success."

Later they even did a national tour and got favorable media attention. "For a bunch of marginalized youth who no one believed in, that was a great thing," said Claudio, who had been in and out of the detention center for his drug use and "stealing problem."

When Claudio and Angel were released from the center, they went to live with Nogales in his tiny apartment and kept working with the theater. But they still both were suffering from serious drug addictions, and about five years after first meeting Nogales Claudio left Teatro Trono to focus on conquering his demons.

"For me marijuana was a door to other drugs, cocaine and crack," he said. "Kicking a drug addiction is a long process. But I had a religious experience that changed me into a different person." He was able to kick his habit at a faith-based rehab center in Santa Cruz called Mission Peniel. He started working at the center, counseling drug and alcohol addicted people of all ages. And he reconnected with Nogales.

"He had known nothing of me for four years," Claudio

said. "We cried on the phone. For him it was like I had returned to earth."

Angel, now 28, also ended up at Mission Peniel, first as a patient and now as a counselor like Claudio. The two maintained sporadic contact with Teatro Trono, and in 1999 they went to Germany and Holland on a tour funded by European arts organizations. Claudio is a natural actor, lithe and animated with dark expressive eyes. Angel, stockier and quieter, lets Claudio get away with playful big brother bullying but then lets fly with a clever quip when least expected. Today they still live and work at Mission Peniel in Santa Cruz and don't have a lot of contact with Teatro Trono. But they are using what they learned to start a theater group with street kids at the mission.

"Theater comes naturally to kids who live on the street," noted Claudio. "They're really expressive, they talk a lot."

Claudio, who is also studying theology, doesn't think poverty alone is to blame for the huge numbers of drug addicted kids on the streets of Santa Cruz, La Paz or other cities. "It's a lack of love," he said. "A person who is addicted to drugs or alcohol—or chocolate—is looking for love. When I found God I had an encounter with love, and my real identity started to emerge little by little and my addictions dropped away. But it's hard to do this. Of the people who come to the mission, 10 percent succeed and 90 percent go back to the streets."

The difficulty of dealing with addictions is one of the reasons Teatro Trono has shifted away from working with street youth and become more of a community-based arts organization serving the children of El Alto. They still do outreach programs to several institutions serving street kids, but the bulk of their work is centered around an amazing seven-story arts center a block from the market in the Ciudad Satelite neighborhood of El Alto. Nogales and other theater members built the center over a five year period. It is also home to COMPA, another arts organization Nogales founded offering classes in ballet, music, ceramics and other pursuits. The center rises above all the nearby buildings like a surreal and whimsical playhouse, odd angles and materials fused together flawlessly, splashed with a myriad of colors and decorated with various baubles and sculptures. The building is made of almost all recycled materials, including windows scavenged from demolition sites and colorful aluminum doors from the micro-buses that careen around El Alto.

"Recycling materials is part of our whole philosophy," noted Coral Salazar. "We believe there's no such things as trash."

A square atrium runs vertically up the center of the building, multi-colored concrete stairs spiraling up around it past a ballet studio, a film screening room, various offices and guest rooms and finally a rooftop garden/ laundry space.

On an afternoon in early March 2004, Nogales, wearing his trademark wide-brimmed hat and always quick with jokes and hugs for the kids, calls a group together for a photo shoot. About 20 youth take over the rooftop in a flurry of circus and theater gear and costumes. Glittery wigs and clown noses go on as Nogales circulates among the kids snapping photos, which will be used in their ever-pressing campaign to get funding from foreign organizations. The photo shoot moves to the street, where the entrance is guarded by an elaborate anthropomorphic sculpture made out of scrap metal. The kids spill out onto the street and the sculpture, climbing it and each other.

"I love theater, it's beautiful," says 13-year-old Gimena, a freckle-faced relative of Nogales.

"It makes you lose your fear," says Christina, 13. "I'm going to be a movie star," proclaims Lito, a scrawny boy who has spent the whole afternoon striking jaunty poses while twirling a green Chinese plate.

Founding member and current circus instructor Gustavo Analoca gets into full clown get-up and face paint for some photos juggling and riding a unicycle. He notes that the puffy short-legged outfit he's wearing was adopted from the Spanish conquistadors, but he adds a Bolivian wool hat for an indigenous touch.

Youth at the orphanage Ciudad del Niño Jesus in La Paz learn circus skills from Teatro Trono. Photo by Kari Lydersen.

In the one-room apartment he shares with his wife and one-year-old son a few blocks from the Teatro Trono center, Analoca has a suitcase and boxes jammed with circus gear—a multitude of glittery and satiny outfits he's made himself, special balloons and a pump to make balloon animals, a unicycle and a collection of pins, balls and other toys. He first picked up circus techniques from a French instructor visiting Teatro Trono, and then doggedly continued to teach himself the art of circus by studying video tapes from around the world, ranging from campy 1970s fare to modern works by Cirque du Soleil. He has been on local television himself doing performances and work-shops at the Arcoiris (Rainbow) center for street youth. When he puts this video on the black and white T.V., his son stops what he is doing and stares at it entranced.

Though he likes working with Teatro Trono, Analoca longs to start his own circus school for marginalized youth in El Alto.

"That would be a great thing for the kids and for Bolivia, because there aren't really any circus schools in Bolivia," he notes. He said there are several traveling family circuses, but they are the old-fashioned type with animals and sensational acts. He prefers the Cirque du Soleil model which eschews ani-mals and slapstick violence in favor of artistry and acrobatics.

"Circus is an option for making a living, and it's a way to motivate you and open your mind," he said while balancing a unicycle on his lap in a crowded mini-bus on the way to Ciudad del Niño Jesus, the La Paz orphanage where he lived for eight years as a child and now teaches circus classes. "In a normal life you're born, go to school, to university if you're lucky, start working in an office. Circus offers a different kind of life. You get to travel, perform, meet different types of people."

At Ciudad del Niño, a beautiful complex of dormitories, classrooms, gardens and even pig pens on a eucalyptus-lined hillside overlooking La Paz, it is evident he is taking the first step in opening a new world for some of the boys who live there.

At the Catholic-run institution funded by the government and several foreign embassies, boys age five and older who are orphans or whose families can no longer take care of them learn trade skills and run small for-profit enterprises including a metal workshop and bakery. During one of his Sunday visits, Analoca plays a video of Cirque du Soleil's "Dralion" for about 30 boys, who sit mesmerized by the fantastic gymnastics and tricks of the performers. The second Analoca turns the video off, the boys swarm over to the buffet of circus equipment which he has laid out in the corner.

Moments later, they are off in a cloud of tossed and dropped hyper-color rings, rubber pins, tennis balls, scarves, big yellow flags and plastic Chinese plates. The pink unicycle draws a rotating crowd in the corner, where no one seems able to launch it without the help of the wall. Manuel, 9, with a runny nose and a scar on his face, moves from one piece of equipment to another seemingly intent on mastering them all. Miguel, also 9, spends the whole time with a yellow Chinese plate, grinning widely as he learns new moves, tossing it in the air and passing it under his leg. Sixteen-year-old Rodolfo, freckle-faced and one of the biggest kids there, is shy at first but then gets wrapped up in the challenge of balancing and twirling sticks.

Analoca hits play on a boombox he has schlepped across the city along with the unicycle and other toys. Soaring, almost operatic music with the refrain "Alegria" ("Happiness") comes out, creating a transcendental scene where any thought of poverty or loneliness is lost in the smiles and laughter of the boys and the flying colors of the circus.

For more information:

COMPA/ Teatro Trono: compain@yahoo.com, evetulbert@msn.com

Fundación Solon: www.funsolon.org

Ciudad del Niño Jesus: www.ciudaddelnino.com

*Part II*

# THE BORDER

A sign in the border town of Falfurrias, Texas, boasts of drug and "alien" seizures. Photo by Kari Lydersen.

Border towns like Tijuana are known for their cheap drugs and trinkets. Photo by Kari Lydersen.

The U.S.-Mexico border is 1,989 miles long, stretching from San Ysidro, California to Brownsville, Texas on the U.S. side and from the cities of Tijuana to Matamoros on the Mexican side.

It is many things to many people.

To U.S. citizens, the border is often a place of cheap thrills and seedy fascination. They cross it to get to cities like Tijuana, Juarez and Nogales where they can cut loose, binging in a way they would never do at home. As memorialized in the Manu Chao song "Welcome to Tijuana, tequila, sex and marijuana," it is a bazaar of illicit drugs, sexual services and cheap liquor.

It is a place for "cheap" things in general—those less intent on partying are likely to cross the border for the bargain souvenirs: polyester striped blankets, ceramic chiles, chintzy sombreros and other trinkets. The streets of border cities are also lined with brightly lit pharmacies, often three or four to a block, garishly advertising "We speak English" and draped in American flags. Here prescription drugs, contacts, crutches and the like can be bought over the counter much cheaper than in the U.S. You can hardly turn your head without seeing a sign for Viagra, and the suspiciously high number of "veterinary" pharmacies are actually outlets for illegal steroids.

Meanwhile, to Mexicans with U.S. citizenship or legal residency, crossing the border is often part of a daily routine. They may live in Mexican border cities to take advantage of the cheaper housing prices, and cross every morning to work in retail, landscaping or food service in the U.S. Or Mexicans living in U.S. border towns will cross every weekend to visit family and do their shopping in Mexico.

For the millions of undocumented Latin American immigrants in the U.S., the border is a far more fearsome and problematic thing. They crossed it to get into the U.S.; in fact they may have crossed it numerous times between deportations before really making it into this country. Now they have to re-cross it every time they want to visit loved ones back home, never knowing for sure if they will make it back to the U.S. and at what expense and risk.

To anti-immigrant groups like the Civil Homeland Defense organization based in Tombstone, Ariz., the border is an embarrassment to the country, an unsecured frontier where foreigners routinely "break in" to the U.S.

To immigrant advocates, like Tucson activist Isabel Garcia, the border is an embarrassment to humanity, a false barrier created to enforce class differences and racial divisions and maintain a constant core of easily exploitable cheap labor in the U.S.

The border can be seen as the epitome of capitalist enterprise—on the macro level with hundreds of millions of dollars worth of goods streaming across and maquilas humming away on the Mexican side making electronics, pharmaceuticals and other goods for export all over the world; and on the micro level, where enterprising traffickers can become rich smuggling drugs and humans across, and lower level hustlers can prey on tourists and thrill-seekers with overpriced baubles and scams.

At some points, like the stretch covering Tijuana, the border is a highly militarized zone, marked by three heavy duty fences, guard posts and search lights with helicopters buzzing overhead.

At other points, it is a muddy river—the Rio Grande or Rio Bravo depending on which side you are on. And at still other areas, it is completely unmarked, not even a line in the dust between cacti.

To those with a shadowy image of the border as a huge barrier, it is amazing to see how simply it can be crossed in many places, by jumping a wall, crawling through a drainage pipe, scurrying through a stretch of desert or showing a borrowed green card or passport at a checkpoint. The real difficulty and danger for undocumented immigrants isn't so much the actual act of crossing the border but the journey to a destination within the U.S. where they can make a living, and the never-ending struggle to find work and avoid deportation that follows.

The border has taken on much greater significance and prominence in the American consciousness since the Sept. 11 terrorist attacks, as U.S. nationalism has swelled and paranoia over national security has mushroomed. The war on terrorism has been used as a major argument for further militarizing the U.S.-Mexico border.

"Since Sept. 11 the country's view of the border has changed from one of just keeping out migrants to a security focus, and that has been really detrimental to the health of everyone at the border," said Rebecca Phares, associate director of the Oblate Justice and Peace Office in Washington D.C. "The work of those of us advocating for more rational policy at the border has been set back five to 10 years at least. There's this atmosphere in the whole country that if the administration even pretends something is connected to national security or anti-terrorism, we'll put up with it."

But the terrorism justification for increased border security doesn't hold up to the most basic scrutiny, when one considers that not a single person convicted of terrorist-related activity entered the U.S. illegally from Mexico. A handful of terror suspects have either entered or tried to enter the U.S. through Canada, yet the Canadian border is twice as long and is not militarized at all in comparison to the Mexican one. As of the summer of 2003 there were about 9,700 Border Patrol agents stationed along the U.S.-Mexico border, and only 1,000 along the Canadian border, even after a 375-agent increase as part of the war on terrorism. A Border Patrol agent interviewed for an Associated Press study said that while people crossing the Mexican border are typically paying about $1,500 to a smuggler, "a terrorist can pay $30,000 or $40,000 and go to the northern border where we don't have the resources to stop them." [88]

While the war on terror may be the current justification for heightened U.S.-Mexico border security, the militarization going on now is just continuing a trend started with Operation Hold-the-Line in El Paso, Texas in 1993, followed by Operation

Gatekeeper in California in 1994, Operation Safeguard in Arizona in 1995 and Operation Rio Grande in Brownsville, Texas in 1997. For the fiscal year beginning Oct. 1, 2003, President Bush had budgeted $9 billion for U.S.-Mexico border security.[89]

In the past few years there has been increased public and media attention to the deaths of migrants crossing the border. With an average of over one death a day in the harsh deserts and mountains, the problem is hard to ignore. (The Mexican government reported that 371 migrants died crossing the border in the 2002 calendar year and at least that many in 2003; U.S. Border Patrol figures are slightly lower.) [90]

The racist violence of anti-immigrant militia groups like Ranch Rescue, including torture and even executions of immigrants, have made for good media coverage, as have the discovery of mass border graves connected to the drug trade. The whole country took notice when, in May 2003, 19 immigrants were found suffocated and cooked to death in the back of an abandoned truck trailer in Victoria, Texas.

But much of the mainstream media coverage of border deaths has missed the point, focusing more on unscrupulous coyotes, vigilante ranchers and cold-blooded drug traffickers as the villains rather than the U.S. immigration and border policy that creates this situation in the first place and allows these characters to thrive.

John Carlos Frey, a Tijuana native who produced and starred in an independent movie called The Gatekeeper about the forced labor of immigrants in methamphetamine labs, regularly points out to his audiences that more people die crossing the border than in the Israeli-Palestinian conflict in any given month; yet one situation dominates the news and the other is barely a blip on the public's radar screen.

He also noted that as he was doing research for his film he was astounded by the lack of media attention given to a rash of immigrant murders.

"Around the time of the sniper attacks (in the Washington D.C. area in 2002) they were finding a body or two a week in Arizona, stripped with the hands tied and shot execution style," said Frey, who makes a living as a soap opera actor in L.A. "They suspected they were trying to escape a drug lab where they were being forced to work. But nobody heard about this. Here they were calling in everyone under the sun to catch the sniper, and these people were being assassinated over a two-month period and getting no press."

There has also been relatively little attention given to the horrors of life on the Mexican side of the border, which are a direct result of the border's existence and enforcement.

As border security has increased, and simultaneously people have gotten poorer throughout Latin America, the crush on the border intensifies.

"The border has always been an escape valve for Mexico," notes Victor Muñoz, a native of Chihuahua who works as a labor organizer in El Paso. "When the border closes it creates more problems in Mexico's border cities. There is more need for social services, more unemployment, water runs out, crime goes way up."

Hundreds of thousands of workers labor in over 3,000 maquilas on the Mexican side of the border, making T.V.s, respirators, auto parts and countless other goods.

Most U.S. natives would find their jaws dropping at the site of the abject poverty in the shantytowns where the workforces of these factories live, shacks constructed out of the trash from these very maquilas. Here kids play in small contaminated streams filled with garbage, in the shadow of the looming, sterile and beautifully landscaped factories where their mothers go to work each day.

Most of them are migrants from other parts of Mexico or Latin America. And while their hometowns were also likely deeply impoverished, at least there they had roots, family and community, maybe even a little land to farm, as opposed to the everyone-for-themselves, cut-throat mentality in the dry dusty borderlands. Many maquila workers came here in hopes of crossing the border, but many of them never will. They will become permanent parts of the swell of humanity pushing up against the border, building more and more hovels in the dry hills that were never meant to sustain this many people; spreading the edges of these cities which never built an infrastructure to handle this size population.

For maquila workers there is little time in a day to make plans to cross the border or do anything else in life.

The group Women on the Border showed that salaries from the maquilas aren't usually even enough to buy a basic basket of food and household items for a small family. For example, a woman would have to work an average of 60 hours in a maquila to earn enough for one school uniform and 11.5 hours to buy a box of 30 diapers (based on average wages of about $3.57 per day in Tijuana maquilas).[91] So many turn to a second shift in the underground economy—drugs or prostitution—in order to put food on the table.

They are also working and living in the toxic residue of the maquila industry, unable to move or get new jobs because bad as they may be these are the best-paying ones around. In Tijuana, the residents of the shantytown known as Colonia Chilpancingo watch babies being born without brains and children growing up with lead poisoning from the detritus of a nearby lead smelter which was closed down by the government in 1993 and never cleaned up.

In Reynosa, young women are getting cancer and mysterious ailments in droves, and they have no doubt the culprit is the chemicals they work with in the maquilas, chemicals which they are often ordered to hide when the government inspectors come around.

Meanwhile in Juarez women maquila workers have something else to worry about—mass murder. Over the past 10 years close to 400 women have been slaughtered in the city, often buried in mass graves with signs of ritual mutilation and rape. Why are they being murdered? There are many theories but no clear answer except that…the murderers can get away with it, enjoying almost total impunity. But thanks to the tireless efforts of mothers of the victims and cross-border activists, this incredible case of femicide has gotten considerable international attention recently.[92]

Unfortunately, as with the public perception of the border deaths, media and government analysis has focused largely on the sensational and specific nature of the murders rather than the systematic root of the problem. Much has been said about the potential involvement of biker gangs, Satanic cults and millionaire sexual deviants. While these culprits may all factor into the equation, the true nature of the problem is both much more obvious and more difficult to address—a political and economic crisis that forces women and families from throughout the country to flee their homes and start a new life, alone and desperate, in one of the most dangerous cities in the hemisphere.

And for those living on the U.S. side of the border life is no picnic either. The border region is one of the poorest regions of the U.S., with inordinately high rates of unemployment, substandard housing, infectious disease and air pollution. Rates of hepatitis A are three times as high and rates of tuberculosis are twice as high along the border as in the rest of the U.S.[93]

Phares sees the health issues along the border both literally and metaphorically.

"A border should be like skin," she said. "A person cannot survive if air can't pass in and out of the skin. To completely seal the border like they're trying to do doesn't promote the health of society."

While people of various races live along the border, a large percentage of the border population are recent or second-generation Latin American immigrants. Like Tijuana and the other Mexican border cities that have experienced population growth way beyond what they are prepared to handle, the population on the U.S. side has also exploded in the past decade. Arizona's border counties saw a 30 percent increase in population between 1990 and 1999, according to Census figures.[94]

Undocumented Latino immigrants living on the U.S. side of the border survive in a constant state of heightened awareness, as they could be deported at any time. Abuses by Border Patrol agents and police in border areas are also commonplace. For example in El Paso in February 2003, a 19-year-old Mexican immigrant named Juan Patricio Peraza Quijada was shot to death by Border Patrol agents in the parking lot of a church that offers services and sanctuary to immigrants—they had stopped to question him as he was taking out the trash, and pursued him when he ran.[95]

Even legal immigrants and U.S. citizens of Latino descent in the border regions are constantly harassed by Border Patrol agents and police, forcing them to carry their green cards or birth certificates at all times.

Thus the border is like a festering seam between these two countries, a place where people come following their dreams and all too often see their dreams crash up against the walls, get snared in the barbed wire and fizzle out in the rubble of the shantytowns. But just as dreams—and people—perish in the cruel border region, so also does hope keep springing up, against all odds, in the form of maquila workers and mothers and teenage boys, shaking their fists at police officers and factory owners and poverty itself; continuing to fight and to hope like the saguaro cacti in the Arizona desert that raise their arms heroically to the desert sky.

Toxic waste eats away at the cement walls and metal barrels on the site of this abandoned lead smelter in Tijuana. Photo by Kari Lydersen.

# CHAPTER SEVEN

# Trashing the Border, Taking Human Lives
## The Residue of Free Trade and Industry in Tijuana

Lourdes Lujan, 30, has spent her whole life in Colonia Chilpancingo in Tijuana.

The community is home to some of the poorest residents of the border city, who live in shacks constructed largely of discards from the maquilas which line the border—wooden pallets, cardboard and plastic molding, rusty mattress springs and pieces of corroded metal from old cars. Many of the shacks have roofs or awnings made from vinyl tarps or banners used for advertising. The words and images on them create a cruel, ironic juxtaposition—the slogans they bear include "Genuine Opportunity," "Quality Inn," "It's Miller Time."

But despite the poverty and inequality all around her, Lujan has happy memories of growing up in Colonia Chilpancingo. The Colonia is centered around a stream, making the area an oasis of lush vegetation in the midst of dusty, dry mesas and plains. The stream runs into the Tijuana River, and then empties into the ocean near the border with the U.S. "We used to come down to the river to bathe and picnic," said Lujan during a visit in June 2003. "The water was clear. It was beautiful."

Since the area is officially declared a flood plain, it is not legal for people to live there. As is the case in different parts of the city, the residents of Colonia Chilpancingo are squatters, living there without legal rights. That means they can't technically get electricity or other services from the government, but with the same ingenuity that helps them create livable shacks out of garbage, the people have rigged up illicit electricity to power televisions and lights. When a flood is expected government officials will clear everyone out of the area, and about every decade a major deluge literally wipes the whole colonia away. But people keep coming back. The government even subsidizes people to get plots of land elsewhere to try to convince them to move out of the flood plain, but Lujan said people end up selling these plots and moving back to Chilpancingo. The main reason, besides the attraction of the stream and vegetation, is that the colonia is less than a mile from an industrial park housing about 130 maquilas. So they can walk to work, saving about a dollar each way on bus fare and avoiding the hour-or-longer commutes that residents from other colonias endure every day. In an industry where the average wage is about $5.50 a day, the savings on bus fare is no small matter.

As the maquila sector has swelled over the past 15 years, Colonia Chilpancingo has grown to about 10,000 people.

And today, the stream is not clear and beautiful. Whitish, oily residue swirls on its surface. Rusted bodies of old cars nestle in the streambed, overgrown with vines, and plastic containers, aluminum cans and other trash float in the water and litter the banks.

But the worst contamination is the kind that can't be seen. This is the contamination that residents blame for causing eight cases of anencephalia and hydrocephalia—babies born without brains or limbs—in a two block area in the past few years. In the U.S., the rate of these birth defects is two per 10,000 people for anencephalia and six per 10,000 for hydrocephalia. Baja California (the Mexican state) is now conducting a study on the state-wide occurrence of these birth defects.[96]

Many residents report that their children lose their hair and bleed from the nose and throat spontaneously. There have been a significant number of cases of leukemia and other fatal, quickly-progressing forms of cancer in the neighborhood. Several residents have mysteriously become ill, had their body parts swell up, and died within months, without ever being diagnosed. There have also been a high number of stillborn babies. And learning disabilities are rampant.

It is hard to scientifically prove what has caused all these maladies. But the residents of Colonia Chilpancingo have no doubt.

They blame the lead, cadmium, arsenic, antimony and other contaminants that are festering on a hilltop just 600 yards or so above the town. This is the former site of the Metales y Derivados plant, a lead smelter which would take boat, car and other batteries from the U.S., separate their components and recycle the lead into bricks to be resold. The factory, owned by U.S. citizen Jose Kahn, began operations in 1972. Right from the start it generated complaints from nearby residents and environmentalists. In 1990 a university study showed the stream running through the town had levels of lead 3,000 times higher than the legal standard in the U.S. and levels of cadmium 1,000 times higher. Residents blamed this contamination partly on Metales, though there is a huge amount of contamination from the industrial park as well. The hair loss, spontaneous bleeding and learning disabilities their children suffer are known effects of lead poisoning.[97]

In 1993 PROFEPA,[98] the enforcement arm of Mexico's version of the Environmental Protection Agency, inspected the plant and shut it down temporarily for numerous violations. Nine months later the agency investigated the plant again and found it had corrected only two of 14 violations, leading to its permanent shut down in 1994. The site was left standing abandoned with over 23,904 metric tons of waste including lead slag, polyethurine chips, sulfuric acid, cadmium and phosphorus. PROFEPA noted there were about 7,000 tons of lead slag alone.[99]

Kahn lives in the U.S., in San Diego's ritzy Point Loma

A mural in Chicano Park in San Diego refers to the toxic legacy of Tijuana and Mexican neighborhoods in San Diego. Photo by Pat Lydersen.

neighborhood. As recently as a few years ago his company New Frontier Trading Corporation continued to operate a plant in California, listing $700,000 to $1 million in sales as of January 1998. Reached at his San Diego home, Kahn refused to comment.

As Kahn has gone on with his life, the Metales plant was left to stand as is, the structure deteriorating over time but the contaminants remaining unmoved.

The physical building is now only a skeleton, with rusted smelting equipment standing like prehistoric beasts inside. Around the skeleton of the building lie huge piles of black battery casings, many with labels indicating they came from El Centro, Calif. or other parts of the U.S. Rusted metal drums are stacked one on top of another, their sides crumbling and eaten through by the chemicals inside. White powder spills out of some of them.

A family—a father, mother and child—actually live in the smelter; some of their clothes and personal belongings are piled next to the stacks of drums. Apparently they have decided life in Tijuana is desperate enough that the contamination is the least of their worries. Or maybe they are not aware of the extent of the risk.

Ironically, the smelter is now overgrown with brilliant sunflowers.

"They don't seem to mind contamination," Lujan said wryly.

The government has made a few futile efforts to cordon off the site. Walls surrounding part of it have been stenciled with the words "Danger: Contaminated Site."

Cement has been poured over part of the area and a cinder block wall has been built around another part. But the relatively new-looking cinder block wall is quickly getting corroded, eaten away as if by acid. It has to be replaced frequently, residents say, since the toxic residue eats through it.

As the deteriorating wall symbolizes, these few efforts at containment are futile. Lead, arsenic and other contaminants permeate the soil and dust in the area. The San Diego-based Environmental Health Coalition (EHC) notes that the contaminants go down at least one to three meters below surface level.[100] When the wind blows across the dry, dusty, sparsely vegetated hillside, it picks up the contaminated soil and carries it down to the colonia. When it rains, contaminated streams flow down the hillside into the colonia.

Along with waste from the 100 plus other maquilas in the industrial park, the byproducts of Metales regularly make their way into the stream that flows through Chilpancingo. For the residents there, there is no way to avoid them. They buy bottled water to drink, but they often bathe and wash with water from the stream. Once a week a truck comes selling slightly-cleaner water for bathing and washing, but it is not enough for all their needs. Even this water they store in discarded barrels from maquilas, laced with lead and other contaminants of their own.

The EHC and a sister committee of Colonia residents, called Colectivo Chilpancingo Pro Justicia Ambiental, is running a campaign to do lead testing on the children of Chilpancingo. So far, they have tested 20 children under age six—the tests cost about $26 each. Every child has tested positive for notable levels of lead, ranging on a scale from 3 to 9. While 10 is considered the danger level by the U.S. Centers for Disease Control, a study published in the *New England Journal of Medicine* noted that levels of 7.4 are known to cause reduction in intellectual capacity and other problems.[101]

"Learning disabilities are really bad, they're one of the biggest problems here," said Lujan. "But if children aren't actually dying the government doesn't care. They don't realize that our children's futures are being stolen by this problem."

"The best way to prevent lead poisoning is to keep your home very clean," said EHC staff member Magdalena Cerda. "But with all the dust that is impossible. And we need to use the water."

As bad as it is, Metales is just one part of the problem.

Lead testing done by the EHC has shown many people have high levels of lead in their kitchen cookware and in the paint on their walls. Studies have even shown that popular juices and candy also contain lead. One of the EHC's campaigns has been to publicize the fact that tamarind candies of the brand Dulmex and other specific candies are known to contain lead. They urge residents to eliminate this candy from piñatas used at Christmas time or during other celebrations.

These sources of lead in daily life aside, it is the contamination from the maquilas that causes the most concern.

In a city that has expanded from less than half a million in 1980 to 1.2 million in 2000 to meet the demand for labor in the maquilas, without a proportional development of city infrastructure and services, there is little attention given to environmental safety and health. Much of the population lives in colonias like Chilpancingo that, while they provide a crucial part of the transnational economy, are largely ignored by the government and multinational companies.

Meanwhile the maquilas, mostly U.S. or other foreign-owned companies like Sanyo, Hitachi and Hyson, do gorgeous landscaping of their own in the industrial park. Someone driving through this area would think they are in a comfortable neighborhood in southern California, never guessing that half a mile away people are living in cardboard shacks and bathing in a contaminated stream.

Despite the lack of a clean water source in Chilpancingo, sprinklers run throughout the day watering the flowering plants around the maquilas.

NAFTA regulations actually stipulate that the waste from maquilas must be returned to the country of their origin-in this case the U.S.

In 2002 the North American Commission for Environmental Cooperation (CEC), an advisory committee formed to deal with environmental complaints under NAFTA, did a report documenting contamination at the Metales site and calling it a "severe hazard to human health." But it did not recommend any specific plans or funding for cleaning up the site, leading environmentalists to call the NAFTA environmental protections a toothless system.

Since neither the CEC nor the Mexican government have made any clean-up plans for the site, the Colectivo and EHC commissioned their own plan, which gives specific directions for a clean-up it estimates would cost $7.2 million and take 90 to 180 days.

On May 14, 2003 the EHC and Colectivo sent a letter to Mexican President Vicente Fox and Victor Lichtinger, secretary of natural resources, outlining the plan and demanding the site be cleaned up to comply with Mexican law and NAFTA provisions.

"This clean-up plan is one of the most simple from a point of view of technical viability, and it is formulated on the principal of the least risk after the cleanup," says the plan prepared by the coalition.[102]

Metales y Derivados is just one example of the constant barrage of toxins that the thousands of maquila workers in cities along the Mexican border are exposed to every day. Like the residents of Chilpancingo in Tijuana, workers in the border cities of Reynosa, Juarez, Matamoras, Nuevo Laredo and other maquila zones also suffer from extremely high incidences of health problems and birth defects because of the toxic material used in the maquilas and the lack of adequate government or private regulation of their use.

But in a cash-strapped country like Mexico, progress is always a struggle. The government doesn't want to anger the owners of the maquilas, which make up such a large part of the economy along the border, and there is little funding for clean-up of environmental hazards like the Metales plant.

The Mexican government and Kahn himself have actually applied for an $800,000 loan from the North American Development Bank to help them clean up the site in compliance with NAFTA terms, but it is unclear whether the loan will be given and that amount would likely not come close to covering the whole clean-up.

Environmentalists note the irony that while the government can't seem to find money for the clean-up of Metales, under the Section 11 provisions of NAFTA, in 2000 Mexico agreed to pay $16.7 million to a U.S. company, Metalclad, to settle a claim that the residents of a town in San Luis Potosi unlawfully prevented the company from building a waste disposal plant there.[103]

Section 11, also called "investor to state dispute resolution," actually allows companies to sue governments for what they allege is interference with their private enterprise rights. Already it has been used in several high profile cases in Canada, the U.S. and Mexico to undermine government attempts to enforce environmental protections. The watchdog group Public Citizen says that under Section 11, "If a corporation wins its case, it can be awarded unlimited amounts of taxpayer dollars from the treasury of the offending nation even though it has gone around the country's domestic court system and domestic laws to obtain such an award."[104]

The residents of Chilpancingo see this as just another example of the kind of double standard they and other impoverished workers in the global economy experience every day.

"If all these toxics were a few meters from Mr. Kahn's house, I'm sure he would have cleaned it up," remarked Andrea Pedro Aguilar, a Chilpancingo resident whose children have suffered severe health problems from lead poisoning. "This is environmental injustice."

For more information:

The Environmental Health Coalition, www.environmentalhealth.org.

Pink crosses adorned with plastic flowers mark the spots where murdered women's bodies were found in the dusty hills of Juarez. Photo by Kari Lydersen.

# CHAPTER EIGHT

# Las Desaparecidas
## The Lost Women of Ciudad Juarez

The desert sand ripples around the bases of the eight pink wooden crosses, adorned with plastic roses, on the hill above the colonia of Anapra in Ciudad Juarez.

They stand like sentinels, across from a fence made of mattress springs, looking out over the sprawling collection of shacks constructed from tar paper, old wooden pallets and plastic crates discarded from the maquilas where most of the Anapra residents work.

The main traffic on the pitted, dusty dirt road curving by the crosses are the rattling, colorful buses—discarded school buses from the U.S.—that come each day around 5 a.m. and again around 2 p.m. to take residents to their maquila shifts. There's a joke circulating in the area that if you want to find Ciudad Juarez, you just follow the crosses.

And there are a lot of them.

These eight pink crosses commemorate some of the women whose bodies were found over the past few years in shallow graves in the dusty hilltop soil. Their bodies were found raped, mutilated and mangled. And they are far from the only ones.

Since 1993, over 350 women, most of them young maquila workers, have disappeared in Ciudad Juarez. The government lists at least 271 as official murders, though residents say the true number is likely well over 400. Of the cases listed by the state government, 178 are listed as cases of domestic violence, with a jealous husband or lover to blame, while 93 are considered the work of a "serial killer" or killers of disputed and unknown identity.[105]

A report by Amnesty International states that in 10 years "approximately 370 women have been murdered of which at least 137 were sexually assaulted prior to death. Furthermore, 75 bodies have still not been identified."[106]

Regardless of the specific numbers, it is clear that they are all part of the same phenomenon—a decade-long wave of hatred and brutality toward women in Juarez, characterized by its gut-wrenching perversity and the failure of the state, local and federal governments to take any meaningful steps to stop the killings or bring justice to the killers.

The bodies have been found one at a time or in groups of three, four, eight. On February 17, 2003, the bodies of three young women were found together and then a six-year-old girl's body was found a few days later. There are nipples, eyes and hearts cut out...signs of brutal rape and other forms of torture. Some were burned to a crisp, others left unburied to be decimated by the harsh desert elements. Some of the victims were buried wearing the clothing of other victims.

They range in age from a three-year-old to an 80-year-old, but the bulk of them were young women between age 14 and 27. Many of them were described as having similar characteristics—tall, thin, lighter-skinned and attractive. A high number of them disappeared in the course of their work at the maquilas, the over 400 companies, 80 percent of them U.S.-owned, that have made this desert city a hub of international commerce. They disappear while waiting for or leaving the buses that take them to and from work, or after visiting the bars that are popular with maquila workers on Friday nights.

Rumors abound as to who is responsible for the scores of unsolved killings.

In 1995 the government arrested an Egyptian chemist named Abdel Latif Sharif Sharif, who had been deported from the U.S. after serving time in jail for sex crimes. The murders continued after Sharif's incarceration, however. He was held for years without a conviction until recently being sentenced to 20

One of the buses that take women to work in Juarez's maquilas. Many of the murdered women were abducted while waiting for the bus. Photo by Kari Lydersen.

years for one of the handful of murders he has been charged with. Then the government blamed and detained members of a street gang called Los Rebeldes (The Rebels), with names like "El Pollo" (The Chicken) and "El Conejo" (The Rabbit).

They claimed Sharif was paying the gang to keep killing women, maybe in an attempt to prove he wasn't to blame for the earlier killings. The authorities claimed he would pay men for bringing him the victim's panties. Sharif's attorneys scoff at this claim, saying Sharif is a scapegoat for the government's unwillingness to truly investigate the murders. Most people on both sides of the border agree.

Rather than Sharif, they blame drug dealers, organ traffickers, sex offenders from the U.S. or Mexican government officials and police officers themselves for the killings. Journalist Diana Washington Valdez has announced that a small group of politically connected American and Mexican millionaires are purchasing the women as sex slaves and then murdering them after acting out their violent fantasies. Like most people who have investigated the murders, she notes that the killers hunt specifically for women who are made virtually anonymous by their poverty, young age and lack of extensive family connections.[107]

A government roster of the victims lists many of them as unidentified—even though in some cases a specific person was charged with their murder. They are listed as "femenino desconocido" or "femenino no identificado"—unknown or unidentified woman. This is the way many of them were thought of in life as well as in death. The young women who work in the maquilas are like cogs in the machine of global commerce. They are expendable and interchangeable, putting in 45 hours or more per week at low-skill assembly line jobs for average pay of $24 to $35 per week, depending on the fluctuation of the peso. These are women who have streamed into Juarez from destitute towns and rural areas in central and southern Mexico.

Marchers went from El Paso to Ciudad Juarez on International Women's Day 2003, demanding "Ni una mas!" ("not one more") death. Photo by Kari Lydersen.

Like in Tijuana, this influx of migrants to a virtually water-less town without the infrastructure to handle such population increases has resulted in the growth of the sprawling colonias, like Anapra on the outskirts of the city. Fifty percent of the roads in the colonias are unpaved, 30 percent of the residents don't have running water and at least 100,000 have no electricity.[108]

Maquilas started popping up in Juarez in the mid-1960s, originally started as a way to use the labor of male Mexican workers returning from the U.S. after the end of the bracero guest-worker program. U.S. and international companies, encouraged by the local and federal Mexican government, realized there was money to be made by harnessing low wage labor across the border to assemble goods for cheap transport back to the U.S. and around the world. Among the many maquilas currently operating in Juarez are Lear, Johnson and Johnson, Honeywell, Avon Automotive and Emerson.

While the maquilas were originally intended to employ men, managers soon realized that it was in fact young women who made the perfect employees. They are considered more docile and obedient, and their young nimble fingers are better-suited to the repetitive work. By the 1980s, about 90 percent of maquila workers were women. More men have become employed in the past decade, with the institution of maquilas making auto parts and other things requiring heavier lifting. But women still make up a sizable 58 percent of the approximately 230,000-person maquila workforce in Juarez.

Sexual harassment and abuse against women in the maquilas is rampant. Women have virtually no choice but to submit to this ongoing harassment, abuse and even rape to hold onto and advance in their jobs. Since the government mandates 60 days of paid leave for pregnant women, maquilas force women to take pregnancy tests and don't hire anyone who is pregnant. Former workers say that in many cases, these "pregnancy tests" consist of showing their used sanitary napkins to managers.

"All the corporations have the same code of conduct—sexual harassment, mandatory pregnancy tests, poor working conditions, humiliation," said Veronica Leiba, a former maquila worker and labor organizer.

Many women are also forced to resort to prostitution or dancing in bars because of the impossibility of supporting a family on maquila wages.

This climate makes the rapes, sexual mutilations and murders more understandable. In everyday life, women are regularly treated as objects of manual labor and sexual gratification for men. That they would meet their deaths that way, and that no one in a position of power would even seem to care, is just the next step.

Up until several years ago, Rosario Acosta was not an activist. But then her 12-year-old niece was murdered. While her young niece was not a maquila worker, the murder led Acosta to become obsessed with the mass murders of maquila workers and other young women. Today, she dedicates herself full time to the struggle to stop the murders and end the impunity enjoyed by many of the killers. She heads the group Nuestras Hijas de Regreso a Casa (May Our Daughters Return Home) out of a small office in Juarez. Acosta has testified in front of the Organization of American States in Washington D.C. and met countless times with local, state and federal government officials demanding action. Since hearing the testimony of Acosta and others, in 2002 the Interamerican Court of Human Rights launched an investigation into the killings and requested accountability from the Mexican government. While this was a welcome step, family members of the victims aren't holding their breath.

"It's promising, but at the same time it's all caught up in bureaucracy," said Acosta. "Meanwhile women continue to disappear. The government wants to hide the problem. The attorney general and the prosecutors are just reducing these lives to numbers. They don't really recognize what's going on, the pain

The mother of one of the murdered women speaks out in Juarez on International Women's Day 2003. Photo by Kari Lydersen.

and suffering of the families, the impact it has on every family in this crisis."

The government has appointed a string of special prosecutors to investigate the killings, but like Acosta, most victims' families, other maquila workers and many in the general public feel the government is not taking even the most basic steps to adequately investigate and prevent the killings.

"Over 300 women have been murdered in Juarez, and no serious investigation is being done," said Texas State Senator Eliot Shapleigh at a rally in El Paso, just across the border from Juarez, on International Women's Day, March 8, 2003.

In April 2003 the Mexican federal attorney general's office decided not to launch a special investigation of the killings, arguing there wasn't evidence that three or more people were orchestrating the killings. Later the federal government did decide to take jurisdiction over the case, largely because of the suggestion that organ trafficking could be involved. While it may seem shocking that it took over a decade for the federal government to move on the cases, this bureaucratic stonewalling at best and maliciousness at worst has characterized the issue right from the start.

In a documentary produced by filmmaker Lourdes Portillo called "Señorita Extraviada" ("Missing Woman") exploring the killings, mothers of the murdered women describe how police refused to investigate their daughters' disappearances at all, often saying they must have run off with a boyfriend. This was the case with Maria Isabel Nava, who was reported missing on Jan. 4, 2000. The special prosecutor's office insisted she must be off with her boyfriend and refused to investigate. Her body was found 23 days later, with evidence that she had been held alive in captivity for about two weeks before being killed.

"When women report their daughter has disappeared, the police respond by challenging the families to convince them of the importance of doing a search," said Acosta. "The police ask personal questions—did she have a boyfriend, was she planning to go out. They say the girls weren't careful enough."

In the maquilas and colonias of Juarez, many believe police and government officials themselves are responsible for the killings.

"It's the police doing it, that's why they won't investigate," said a 25-year-old male cafeteria worker at the Lear maquila after a shift in early March 2003. "That's what everyone thinks. They say people get paid to bring them women, 500 pesos (about $50 U.S.) for each woman."

In "Señorita Extraviada," a woman describes being raped and abused while in police custody. She says the police showed her photos of mutilated bodies in the desert, and threatened that she would be next if she reported her rape.

The explanation the police and government, including the governor of the state of Chihuahua, often give for the killings is that the women were involved in prostitution or drug trafficking, and that they shouldn't have been out at night.

In February 1999, the former State Public Prosecutor, Arturo González Rascon, stated that, "Women with a nightlife who go out very late and come into contact with drinkers are at risk. It's hard to go out on the street when it's raining and not get wet."[109]

Of course going out to bars for fun or working in clubs or as a prostitute can hardly be considered grounds for a gruesome death sentence, the sentence the prosecutor is essentially defending.

And his statements also ignore the fact that some of the women were abducted in broad daylight. Others are forced to be out alone in the dark because their maquila shifts end at 12:30 a.m. or they have to catch 5 a.m. buses in the morning.

"The maquila owners say the reason they're getting killed is they're wearing those short skirts and going dancing," said Victor Muñoz, a member of an El Paso-based coalition against the killings. "It's the attitude of blaming the victim."

Advocates say efforts to get the maquilas to provide more

security for women on their way to and from work have gone nowhere.

"We've raised the issue of safety with the maquilas, but they keep telling us they're doing everything they can and there's nothing more they can do," said local labor organizer Beatriz Lujan.

On a larger level, many see the murders as part of an overall culture that wants to keep women subservient and dependent on men. This includes both the maquila owners who want their female employees to be docile and obedient, and husbands who want their wives to be the same way.

As rough as working conditions in the maquilas are, they have given women a newfound sense of independence and economic freedom. In their hometowns, women usually wouldn't have had the freedom to go to bars alone or work alongside and socialize with men.

Women say there is general resentment from men at the fact women are earning money on their own and taking jobs in a tight economy. Overwhelming and increasing poverty just exacerbates these feelings.

"There are a lot of problems for poor people in Juarez," said Esther Chavez Cano, founder of Casa Amiga, the only domestic violence crisis center in the city. "Jobs are being lost at the maquilas and the maquilas are paying less. Domestic violence increases, alcoholism has increased tremendously. In our culture men feel they are supposed to be the supporters of the family, and they are frustrated that the women are earning the money, so they abuse more."

The recession in the U.S., and corporations' growing interest in even cheaper labor in Asia, has had a significant effect on the maquila industry in the past few years. Yet economic conditions in the rest of Mexico continue to worsen as well, so the stream of workers up to Juarez continues. This squeeze threatens to make the violence against women even worse. With more competition for jobs, maquilas will have even less incentive to provide decent working conditions, wages and security measures for workers.

"The maquilas are not trying to create better conditions, and workers' frustration is increasing," said Leiba. "This is a time bomb waiting to go off."

The situation is not limited to Juarez, either. Over the past three years at least 16 women have disappeared in Chihuahua City, about five hours south of the border. Like the Juarez victims, most of them were young maquila workers. As with the Juarez murders, the police investigations of the cases have been characterized by gross misconduct and neglect. For example, after Neyra Azucena Cervantes was reported missing in May 2003, police did no investigation. Then after her body was discovered two months later, her cousin and father were detained for questioning. Her cousin was later charged with the murder, but like some of the suspects in the Juarez killings he reported being tortured into signing a pre-written confession.

As terrifying and frustrating as the situation may be, family members and activists are not without hope.

A variety of women's groups and organizations of the victims' mothers have formed in Juarez to fight for accountability, justice and the prevention of more killings. Coalitions have also been formed with U.S. groups near the border and major U.S. foundations have funneled financial resources to the struggle. The event on International Women's Day in 2003 drew about 500 people marching through El Paso and Juarez, demanding an end to the murders and violence against women in general. Over the Day of the Dead weekend (Oct. 31 -Nov. 2, 2003), Amnesty International and the Chicano Studies Research Center at UCLA hosted an international conference about the killings, where family members, scholars and activists from around the world came together.

At a March 2003 reading by Sergio Gonzalez Rodriguez, author of a book about the killings, distraught audience members from El Paso and Juarez came together.

They described the struggle as not just a search for justice for past victims and for the safety of potential victims, but as a symbol of the well-being and hope of Mexican women as a whole.

"These young women represent the future of Mexico," said one young woman. "And they are being killed. That is a metaphor for the future of Mexico."

For more information:

Mexico Solidarity Network, www.mexicosolidarity.org.

Amnesty International, www.amnestyusa.org/women-/juarez.

Casa Amiga, www.casa-amiga.org.

Nuestras Hijas de Regreso a Casa, www.geocities.com/por-nuestrashijas.

Members of the democratic workers committee DODS fight for better pay and conditions in the maquilas in Reynosa. Photo by Kari Lydersen.

# CHAPTER NINE

# Poisonous Profits
## The Malignant Underside of Reynosa's Maquila Zone

To Grace Katia Elvira Lara Delgadillo, it was worth it to work close to 100 hours a week repairing electronic parts for autos for Delphi Corp., a spin-off company from General Motors in Reynosa, Mexico just across the border from McAllen, Texas.

Grace started working at the Delphi maquila in 1997, at age 17. Earning double and sometimes triple pay for overtime, bringing her wages somewhat above the average $5 to $8 a day that maquila workers earn, she was able to buy furniture, a refrigerator and even a washing machine for her mother.

Little did she know the price she and her family would pay for her dedication. Or rather she could have known, or at least guessed, given the experiences of countless other women (and men) who worked at Delphi, which is also known locally as Delnosa, and other maquilas. But since there was no other economically viable alternative for a young woman in Reynosa, it was easier not to think about it.

Sitting in her small but comfortable concrete-walled home on a summer afternoon in 2003, Grace's older sister Aneth and her twin sister Heidi described how Grace's illness started.

The warning signs started with rashes on her arms and hands, nosebleeds, fatigue and persistent throat infections. In January 2002 she had a miscarriage, followed by profuse bleeding that required a blood transfusion. Her health worsened over the spring and summer and she was fired from Delnosa for missing too much work. She briefly got hired somewhere else so she could get health coverage—in Mexico, anyone who is working gets government-provided health care for themselves and their dependents but those who aren't working in the formal economy are out of luck.

On December 12, 2002, Grace suffered a brain hemorrhage that left her paralyzed on one side. Her family wanted to take her to Monterrey, some hours drive away, for the top medical care. But since it was the holidays it was difficult to get an appointment, and they feared she might not survive the long drive. In Reynosa, meanwhile, it was also hard to get care since she wasn't working by this point—they had to take her from clinic to clinic and scrounge for money to get doctors to see her.

In late December Grace ended up having open cranial surgery and later that month she suffered another stroke. On January 3, 2003, Grace Katia Elvira Lara Delgadillo was dead. Her death certificate listed cancer, of a duration of six months, and brain hemorrhage as the causes.

There is really no way to prove what caused Grace's illness and death, but the testimonies of countless maquila workers and scientists over the years would indicate that one likely cause was her daily exposure to toxic substances including lead, toluene, conformol and other paints and solvents at Delnosa, where she had worked almost every day for almost six years.

Spontaneous bleeding, fatigue and vomiting are all known effects of lead poisoning, and toluene and other chemicals used in the plant are known carcinogens.

Delnosa workers note that they are given a brief lecture on safety and toxic chemicals when they start work at the plant, and are forced to sign a statement saying they have gone through this so-called safety training. But after that, they are never given updated or repeated information or warnings about the chemicals.

Aneth said Grace's latex gloves would often tear or break, and she was slow to replace them since the worker had to pay for new gloves.

"She never knew all this work would cause her harm," said

Aneth, 28. "With all the overtime, she didn't have time to detoxify her body. The workers are all exposed to so many chemicals. The protections in the plant are all to protect the product and the machinery, but they don't care at all about us."

Now Grace's sister Heidi is also suffering health problems she thinks are related to her work. She works at a plant that makes automatic insulin injection devices for diabetics. She thinks something used to make the glue that affixes the devices to the body is toxic. It causes her skin to turn white and grainy.

"I don't know what it is," she said. "They don't tell us anything."

Ed Krueger, a veteran cross-border organizer and former minister who helped Aneth and other local workers start a workers' rights committee called Derechos Obreros Democracia Sindical (DODS), thinks methylene chloride or another solvent might be to blame for Heidi's white hands.

"That's very bad because it takes all the oil out of the skin, turning it white, and then the toxins are absorbed even faster," he said.

When Grace's family went to Delnosa demanding financial assistance and information during her sickness, the company denied that Grace had ever worked there. Never mind the numerous company photo IDs from various years that her family has on hand.

While dealing with the pain of Grace's death, and the large medical bills they have been saddled with, Grace's family are not taking her death quietly. They are determined to hold someone accountable and to prevent others from suffering the same fate. Her sister Aneth is studying to be a lawyer and also working as the secretary of DODS. She takes every opportunity to hand out files of paperwork relating to her sister's case—her medical records, death certificate and copies of her Delphi IDs. Along with bringing some closure to her sister's case, she wants to let other women know about the critical danger they are putting themselves in by daily handling toxic chemicals and breathing toxic fumes in the maquilas. "It's not just my sister," she said. "Many people are in the same situation."

For example, there is Maria Jimenez (who asked that her real name not be used). Maria is 34. For eight years she has also worked at Delnosa. Like Grace, a year or two ago she started suffering severe fatigue, rashes, nosebleeds and throat infections. She was fired last fall for missing too much work. She went to the doctor several times and was told they didn't know what was wrong with her. In March 2003, she was told she had cancer, and that it was very advanced. She said the doctor didn't seem very sympathetic.

"He said, 'You're going to die, if you don't die of cancer you'll die of getting run over by a car or something anyway,'" she remembered during a talk on a late June afternoon in 2003. She was angry at the doctor's flippancy and devastated by the news.

"I thought that before I died of cancer, I'd die of thinking and crying so much," she said. "Everyone dies, but to confront death is very hard. I had all these plans for the future, things I wanted to do with my kids. When I heard I had cancer, even more than myself I thought of my kids."

She struggled to break the news to her children, ages 5 through 16. Her 16-year-old daughter became so distraught that she had a nervous breakdown and became very ill. On March 20, 2003 Maria had emergency surgery to remove a malignant tumor. In the next few months she had 25 or more radiation treatments, and now she goes for nine-hour chemotherapy treatments once a week.

"I feel very tired, my skin is peeling off and yellow fluid comes out of my body," she said, looking amazingly cheerful and vital despite the stress her body was going through.

She has no doubt that working at Delnosa caused her illness. She explains that workers were only allowed three bathroom breaks during their 12 hour shifts—she worked from 5 p.m. to 5:30 a.m.—so they would regularly eat snacks or touch their face and mouth without being able to wash the lead and other toxins off their hands.

"This must have affected us a lot," she said.

She thinks the workers' safety equipment was grossly inadequate.

"We were working with lead solder that caused a lot of smoke," she said. "In front of each worker was a filter with a small fan that would blow the smoke away from the worker, but it would blow it right toward the worker next door. I even went to the union to talk about this because everyone was getting diseases of the nose and throat. But that didn't change anything. While I was there they never did get the tubes that they were supposed to get to suck the smoke out of the factory."

Workers at Delphi are all represented by the CTM union,[110] one of three unions that represents the majority of workers in Reynosa. Like most unions in Mexico, the CTM is considered government-aligned and usually sides with the employer. Aneth says angrily that the union representatives at Delnosa were allied with management or were running for various government positions, so they didn't want to stand up against the company or rock the boat.

"They never do anything to help us," she said.

Like Grace, Maria said she got no help from Delnosa after she became ill. She was even denied a "profit-sharing" bonus which she was due. Under Mexican labor law, companies are supposed to divide 10 percent of each year's profits among their employees. Since foreign-owned maquilas don't report profits in Mexico, they make themselves technically exempt from this law, but workers still expect to get some kind of profit-sharing payment. In 1997, when General Motors owned Delnosa, over 400 workers carried out a work stoppage to demand a profit-sharing payment; GM eventually agreed with a $45 pay-out and $32 in coupons to each employee, according to some of the workers.

In Maria's case, Delnosa was giving profit-sharing to workers, but she said managers told her that since she had been fired in October and hadn't finished the whole year, she wouldn't get the bonus of about 1,500 pesos (roughly $150 U.S.).

Delnosa is one of the largest of about 175 maquilas in Reynosa, employing 4,094 workers in its plants, according to the company's web site (workers say they are told there are 7,600 employees in the company's six local plants.)[111]

Delphi has headquarters in Troy, Mich. as well as Paris, Tokyo and Sao Paulo. Delphi was spun off into an independent company by General Motors in 1998, but General Motors is still its biggest customer. Delphi has 171 manufacturing facilities around the world, with 47 in Mexico and South America. Delnosa alone ships 80,000 products daily to 72 customer locations in 11 countries around the world, according to the Texas-based plant operations manager.

Like Delnosa, a large sector of the maquila industry in Reynosa is devoted to electronic harnesses and other electronic equipment for cars. Household electronics and medical supplies are other big industries. Still other maquilas produce luxury goods that a maquila worker would never dream of owning—for example Kongsberg makes electric seat warmers for luxury cars, Springs Window Fashions makes Venetian blinds and Rey Mex Bra makes high-end lingerie for the Vanity Fair label.

Ironically, on one of the tan-colored, windowless buildings that house Delnosa, in the lavishly landscaped industrial park, there is a huge white banner congratulating Delnosa's employees on the company's winning the Shingo Prize for Excellence in Manufacturing, given by Utah State University, and known as the "Nobel Prize of Manufacturing" in the industry. Utah State's web site notes that Delnosa has increased productivity 34 percent and achieved 100 percent employee participation in "implemented improvement ideas for 2002."[112]

"You don't win prizes, you earn them," said Delnosa spokesman Michael Hissam, who failed to return later calls regarding this story, in a brief interview. "We earned this prize. We're proud of our performance."

But most workers wonder why it doesn't implement ideas that keep them from getting fatal diseases from working with toxic chemicals.

Maria thinks that Delnosa managers know full well that they were and are exposing employees to high levels of toxic chemicals and components on a daily basis. Referring to a government inspection in spring 2002, she describes how managers would tell her and other workers to hide certain things when inspectors came.

"They wouldn't use certain chemicals when the inspectors came, and they would tell us to take all these chemicals and things that had been burned or stained by them and put them in lockers," she said. "And anyone who had throat infections would be told to go in the bathroom. One time I couldn't speak well because I had a sore throat, and they sent me to the bathroom. There were seven of us in there."

Delnosa even coached workers on what to tell inspectors if they were interviewed, according to the workers. Maria and Aneth have copies of sample question and answer sheets the company handed out to the workers. If they were asked "What is ISO14001?" they were to say, "The international standard for a business to minimize its impact on the environment." If they were asked why their company is implementing this standard, they were supposed to answer, "To have a safe workplace to protect the environment and human health, to be competitive and to be known as a company with an environmental conscience."

Accidents are also common at Delnosa and other maquilas. Workers throw around stories about a woman's hair getting caught in machinery and scalping her, fingers cut off by machinery, electrocutions from loose cables. Dafne Cervantes Gonzalez, who works from 5:30 a.m. to 7:30 p.m. at General Electric, notes that the company offers a reward of chocolate for the employees if they go 30 days without an accident, and T-shirts if they go 90 days without an accident.

"But we never get the chocolate—there are so many accidents!" she laughs.

Like many people in Reynosa, Maria is from Veracruz, a state in the lush south of the country on the coast of the Gulf of Mexico. Workers say that about 80 percent of Delnosa employees and the majority of the population of the town as a whole are from Veracruz. The streets of Reynosa are lined with stores or roadside stands advertising cheese from Veracruz or Veracruz-style bread. Most made the journey north because of a lack of opportunity in the poor, agriculture-based state.

"I was a single mother and I needed a way to support my kids, so I came up here," 10 years ago, said Maria, who is from the town of Poza Rica in Veracruz. Like others asked why they came to Reynosa, she seems surprised at the question, as if the migration north is a given part of life.

Leticia Sanchez (who asked that her real name not be used), 49, is another migrant from Poza Rica, Veracruz. Leticia and her husband live in an area known as Colonia Independencia on the outskirts of the city. While many homes closer to the center of Reynosa have concrete walls and floors and store-bought doors and windows, homes in the colonias, the poorest neighborhoods, are cobbled together from the detritus of the maquilas and other found items. To an outsider it is amazing to see the creativity and inventiveness that goes into creating livable homes from wooden pallets, rusted mattress springs, car doors and cardboard.

Leticia's home is surrounded by a beautiful garden of pink and white flowers known as Teresitas and ringed by a fence made from sticks topped with tin cans and other objects. She waters the Teresitas with help from a neighbor, since she has no running water or electricity. Just beyond Leticia's house is a large water-filled gorge that might be beautiful if it weren't filled with cascading piles of bottles, tires, plastic, old mattresses and other trash. The piles of garbage almost seem like organic living things, flowing down the hillsides and mixing with the reeds in the water. Since there is no public waste pick-up, poor residents have no choice but to dump their refuse in places like this.

The streets that curve around the makeshift dump to Leticia's house, like most streets in Reynosa, are unpaved and pitted. Every 15 minutes or so one of the buses that take people to work at the maquilas rumbles by—most of them are old school buses from the U.S. Other than this most people get by on foot, bicycle, or the occasional burro or mule-drawn cart. When it rains, as it frequently does during the first part of the summer, the roads quickly turn into huge mud puddles, better described as milky brown ponds. Children slosh through the mud barefoot and play in the streets as if they were public pools, horsing around and pulling each other in makeshift "boats." Given the lack of sewer systems, this mud and water is a stew of infectious disease—a source of pathogens that could easily be eliminated with a little investment in paved roads and sanitation services by the government or the maquilas where most of the residents work.

Contrary to how it may sometimes seem, there is plenty of hope in Reynosa. Leticia, for example, is full of shy smiles as she describes her recent involvement with DODS. At her age, she had no chance of working in the maquilas, which generally only hire women in their teens and 20s or mid-30s at the oldest. Leticia had been working in a cafeteria serving the Panasonic maquila, but in February 2003 she was arbitrarily given a shift change that made it impossible for her to get to work. She thinks this too was a case of age discrimination.

Krueger visited her with two representatives from DODS— Aneth and Teresa Chavez. They snapped into action filing a complaint with the company. After just one arbitration meeting in May, Leticia was rehired. Now she works from 6 p.m. to 6 a.m. Thursday through Sunday.

Paulina  (who asked her last name not be used) is likewise enthused about DODS. At a restaurant on one of Reynosa's busy streets, with a breeze stirring the otherwise sultry air, Paulina holds up a piece of butcher paper listing the names of different workers and the amount of money DODS has helped them collect in severance pay and other due wages from recalcitrant employers. After 18 and a half years working in the Zenith maquila, Paulina is now a full-time staff facilitator for DODS. Since its founding in 1997, DODS has grown to support five paid staff members and about 100 volunteers. Paulina describes how she, Teresa and other activists waged a battle to force General Motors (which then owned Delnosa) to hire pregnant women in 1997. Paulina notes that even now she often helps workers who were fired for pregnancy at other plants to get hired at Delnosa.

"It's because of pressure from our people that Delnosa changed its policy," Paulina said.

A job at Delnosa might not exactly seem like a benefit given Grace Delgadillo's experience. But workers stress that Delnosa is no worse than other maquilas. Conditions are bad all around, and women are so desperate for work that they are willing to risk exposure to toxic chemicals to put food on the table.

Teresa Chavez, a long-time rabble-rouser who has worked in maquilas in Mexico City and Reynosa since 1980, talks with determination and confidence about the committee's various campaigns and battles. She has a scar on her inner wrist from surgery for carpal tunnel syndrome, caused by having to make a circular motion 518 times an hour to trim excess metal off a fixture at the RBC de Mexico maquila.

She has been involved in work stoppages to get better conditions and pay over the years, and as both a worker and now a DODS staff organizer she is not afraid to take on managers and union officials. She says that she has had strangers enter her home and ask about her organizing activities, and she has received threatening phone calls, but that doesn't stop her. She shows off the official DODS pen, inscribed with their name and address and a picture of an eagle with the words (in English) "Dare to Fly."

"The eagle is a symbol of strength," she said. "That's us."

For more information:

The Comite de Apoyo, Inc., PO Box 1206, Edinburg, TX 78540-1206.

Coalition for Justice in the Maquiladoras:
http://enchantedwebsites.com/maquiladora/cjm.html.

Mike Wilson refills one of the water tanks Humane Borders places in the deadly Arizona desert for migrants. Photo by Kari Lydersen.

The Tombstone Tumbleweed's main mission seems to be to drum up hatred toward immigrants in the small Arizona town. Photo by Kari Lydersen.

# CHAPTER TEN

# Casualties of War
## The Border's Death Zone

It's not Alpha, so it must be beeps or the illegals," says Chris Simcox in a hushed voice, speaking into his walkie talkie from his perch on a small rise in the brushy, dry Arizona desert about a mile north of the U.S.-Mexico border.

By "Alpha," he means one of his compatriots in the Civil Homeland Defense organization that he founded in the fall of 2002, based in Tombstone, Arizona, the home of the infamous OK Corral gun battle.

By "beeps," he means Border Patrol agents; about 1,800 of them patrol this area with helicopters, motion sensors, night vision and other high tech equipment 24 hours a day.

And by "the illegals," he means undocumented immigrants crossing the border from Mexico. Since the borders have been increasingly militarized and in some places effectively sealed in much of California, Texas and Arizona, this strip of desert south of Tuscon has become the most popular place for immigrants to cross—Mexicans as well as Central and South Americans and Asians, Eastern Europeans and even Africans who fly to Mexico en route to what they hope will be a better life in the U.S.

Along with being the most popular place for immigrants to cross the border, it is also the most deadly.

The Border Patrol reports that 320 people died crossing into the U.S. in 2002, from thirst, heat exposure and other problems. And it is likely that many deaths were unreported.[113]

During the winter, more will freeze to death after being caught in sub-freezing temperatures and rain.

Simcox claims that he and the other CHD members who

patrol the desert several times a week are trying to "save lives."

"When we see a group of immigrants, we shine a light on them and say, 'Alto, por favor, sientense,' ('Stop, please, sit down.')," said Simcox, 42, who came to Tombstone from Los Angeles, where he was a teacher at a private elementary school. "Usually they sit down. Sometimes the young males run, and we let them run. This is community service as well as political activism. We have a lot of compassion for these people, especially the women and children."

Simcox's group then calls the Border Patrol, who usually come fairly quickly. Once they come, the immigrants are taken to a nearby detention center, processed, and usually deported back across the border within 48 hours.

Simcox says his group has apprehended 1,750 immigrants between November 2002 and September 2003, including many Mexicans from Puebla and the southern state of Chiapas and Brazilians, Poles and people of other nationalities.

"This summer we encountered 40 plus Chinese with a Mexican smuggler over here," he said, referring to a certain part of the desert as his truck rumbles by. "It's well known that it's an easy ticket into America."

While Simcox touts the number of lives his group has saved, immigrants' rights advocates describe Simcox's group and other civilian patrol groups, like Glenn Spencer's American Border Patrol, which also operates in the area, and Jack Foote's Ranch Rescue based in Abilene, Texas, as vigilante groups who hate immigrants and aren't afraid to take the law into their own hands, sometimes with violent results.

"These vigilante groups chase people with dogs, threaten people with guns, beat people," said Isabel Garcia, a legal aid lawyer in Tucson and a leader of Derechos Humanos, a human rights and immigrants' rights group. "We first encountered them in the '70s and '80s but now they've begun to band together. They issued a declaration to the feds saying if you don' take control of the border, we will, and blood will be shed."

Members of Foote's group have been accused of detaining, torturing and shooting immigrants. On May 29, the Southern Poverty Law Center and MALDEF (the Mexican American Legal Defense Fund) aided six Mexican and Salvadoran migrants in filing a lawsuit against five ranchers or Ranch Rescue members who are accused of imprisoning, violently assaulting, threatening and robbing them. Foote, a Gulf War veteran and perhaps the most virulent of the high-profile vigilantes, has referred to Mexicans as "dog turds" who are "ignorant, uneducated and desperate for a life in a decent nation because the one they live in is nothing but a pile of dog shit made up of millions of little dog turds" in emails obtained by the Southern Poverty Law Center.[114]

Spencer, meanwhile, has installed at least 27 sensors in the ground near the border, which set off alarms in his Sierra Vista home whenever immigrants (or Border Patrol agents or cattle for that matter) walk over them. He has cameras set up to film the immigrants, and posts the images on the internet. He has stated that his goal is to have 500 sensors in place, at a cost of about $350,000, and to purchase an unmanned aerial drone to photograph and locate immigrants.[115] (The Border Patrol has also announced plans to use the unmanned drones, which have been used heavily by the military in Iraq and other recent wars.)[116]

The Southern Poverty Law Center, which lists the patrol groups as hate groups, has documented almost 40 incidents since 1999 in Cochise County (which includes Tombstone and the area Simcox 'patrols') alone in which immigrants were illegally detained, and at least five cases where they were shot or beaten. In October 2002, 35 heavily armed members of Ranch Rescue conducted a hunt for migrants in southeastern Arizona and were investigated in connection with the murder of an immigrant near Red Rock, Ariz., where two masked gunmen opened fire on a group of 12 immigrants napping by a pond.[117] In May 2003 the Border Action Network kicked off a campaign to locate "victims of vigilante violence," noting that Mexican consulates in Arizona had taken reports of 29 incidents of violence against immigrants in the first four months of 2003.[118]

Simcox, 42, started CHD after working as a hired security guard for ranchers and even as a gunslinger in the reenactments for tourists of the battle of the OK Corral.

In August 2003 Mexican officials demanded an investigation of an Aug. 1 incident in which Simcox and other CHD members held 29 immigrants at gunpoint, which is a felony.[119]

However none of the detainees would testify, so no charges were filed. Simcox maintained that the immigrants mistook his group's walkie-talkies for guns. However, the members of Simcox's patrol do carry side arm pistols in holsters on their hips, which is fully legal in Arizona. And his exhortations aside, there are plenty of clues that Simcox and his cohorts aren't exactly fond of immigrants. There is an upside down Mexican flag pinned to the wall in the small desert office that CHD operates out of, with hand-lettered signs saying "No Invasion" and "No Drugs" and a God Bless America sticker on the window. During a night patrol in September 2003 one member of the group, who is known as Two Gun, wears a Savage Nation hat, referring to far-right-wing shock jock Michael Savage, known for his virulent anti-immigrant views.

A note scrawled on a dry erase board in the office mentions a complaint made by an immigrant who felt his civil rights were violated, rights that he "just acquired after squeezing under the border fence."

As the group gets ready to go out on patrol, dressed largely in camouflage or hunting gear, Simcox, wearing a bulletproof vest, says, "Where's the rescue water? It's been a warm day, we need at least two gallons."

The other members don't seem too concerned about finding the water; when only one gallon is found, one jokes, "Oh well, I guess some of them will just have to die."

Simcox has also publicly defended two men charged with

detaining a group of immigrants at gunpoint and assaulting them on July 31, 2003. The group included three children and a 16-year-old smuggler.

Simcox is the editor and owner of The Tombstone Tumbleweed, a local newspaper with all headlines printed in the same Old West font that adorns most of the storefronts and signs in Tombstone. Simcox says he spent all his retirement savings to buy the paper, which bills itself as the voice of "The Town Too Tough To Die," to have an outlet to alert the public about the immigration problem. And every issue of the 12-page paper is dominated by the immigration debate, with a strange mix of concern at the labor exploitation and deaths of immigrants along with what can only be labeled anti-immigrant sentiment. In countless interviews with the press, Simcox has demonstrated a similar schizophrenia—his published quotes range from denunciations of employers who exploit immigrants and declarations of support for hardworking immigrants to outbursts that "They are evil people," as he said in an interview with the Southern Poverty Law Center.

"They are hardcore criminals," he told them. "They have no problem slitting your throat and taking your money or selling drugs to your kids or raping your daughters."[120]

In the July 10, 2003 issue of the Tumbelweed, Simcox issues a "call to arms" for citizens to join him in patrolling the border.

"Where is Uncle Sam when you need him?" the paper asks. "Powerful government officials unable to solve border problems. More citizens needed to assist border patrol. Civil Homeland Defense recruiting new volunteers. Help save lives during the summer of '03."

The September 18, 2003 issue of the Tumbleweed has a front page story about increases in drug smuggling across the border, a story about an anti-immigration protest in North Carolina, and letters defending Simcox —"If a man has the guts to put his livelihood on the line for a cause, by golly shouldn't you be able to stop worrying what your neighbors might think about you?" writes Carmen Mercer. "And Corporate America, you are not helping your country by being greedy and paying cheap labor to illegal immigrants! You are taking away jobs from our own people who have had the education to fill these spots."

(Never mind that "these spots" are mainly low-wage jobs in agriculture, meatpacking, landscaping and industry that most U.S. citizens are unwilling to do, education or no.)

After parking their trucks and jeeps off a dirt trail near the spot where they will set up their patrol for the night, the CHD members point out scores of footprints in the dust and the empty water bottles and other scraps of trash the migrants have left behind.

Among other things, Simcox says, the migrants cause environmental destruction, a charge echoed by many environmentalists who take anti-immigration stances even though they may be to the left of center on other issues.

"They go through national conservation areas, and you should see the environmental damage they leave," Simcox said. "Human feces, feminine sanitary napkins, diapers, these are biohazards."

This night Simcox's shift on patrol is quiet, despite the footprints that show many immigrants made their way through earlier in the day. The group theorizes that maybe coyotes are bringing their groups by in the early morning instead of the night, or maybe they have found a different route.

While Simcox and his friends claim to have compassion for immigrants, they definitely don't want them coming into the country illegally. Simcox would like to see the border completely sealed off with thousands of military police and a support staff of thousands of volunteers like himself.

He blasts President Bush and his immigration policy for allowing immigrants to keep crossing the border illegally.

"It's embarrassing that the greatest superpower in the world can't stop poor immigrants from breaking into our country," he said. "National security is a joke. It's obvious that there's economic oppression going on in Mexico, and it's gotten worse since NAFTA. But we're caught in the middle. The American taxpayer is not supposed to be the social welfare system for all of Mexico. This is a tax revolt."

Isabel Garcia and other immigrants' rights advocates in the Tucson area and around the country are also no fans of Bush's immigration policy. But they have a far different solution in mind than Simcox. They want to see the millions of undocumented immigrants who labor for low wages (often in unsafe conditions) in the U.S. to be given legal residency and full workers' rights. They would also like to see an opening and liberalization of the borders, which seems only natural given that NAFTA and other free trade measures have virtually obliterated any restrictions on the flow of commerce across borders.

"We're living a human tragedy here at the border," said Garcia. "Everyone knows about the Berlin Wall, but we lose more people every year at the U.S.-Mexico border than in the entire history of the Berlin Wall, and it seems like no one knows about it. These are horrible, unnecessary deaths. People have to go through a deadly obstacle course to pick our fruit and make our clothes."

Immigrants started streaming into Arizona in the mid-1990s, after the borders in Texas and California were heavily secured through Operation Gatekeeper in California, Operation Hold the Line in the El Paso area and Operation Rio Grande in South Texas. These operations included the militarization of the borders with increased numbers of agents and high tech surveillance technology, as well as the literal building of walls, many times out of surplus military steel.

In 2002, 40 percent of the Border Patrol's apprehensions were in Arizona, according to the agency. There is a steel wall along the Mexico-Arizona border in the southeastern part of the state, driving migrants into the rough mountainous terrain and harsh weather of the state's West Desert corridor, which is actually roughly in the center of the state. This area is a corridor of death.

But Robin Hoover, pastor of the First Christian Church in Tucson, has dedicated his life to "taking death out of the immigration equation," as he is fond of saying.

In various spots throughout the desert one can see tattered blue flags waving against the equally blue sky, thanks to a group called Humane Borders that Hoover helped found. Below the flags are one to three 65-gallon tanks painted bright blue with the word "Agua" (Water) and a sticker showing the big dipper constellation filled with water and the words "Fronteras Compasivas" (Humane Borders). For the past three years, Hoover's life has revolved around these water tanks, 24 hours a day, seven days a week. Hoover, a friendly Texas native who is always quick with a laugh and a slightly off-color joke, first got involved with immigration issues while working at the country's largest processing center for asylum seekers in Los Fresnos.

When he heard about all the people dying crossing the border, he realized his mission was to stop the deaths. He met with a group of other concerned people in June 2000 at the Quaker meeting house in Pima County, Ariz., "on Pentecost Sunday," Hoover said. "We asked what we could do to provide humanitarian assistance to the people crossing the desert, and what can we do to change the policies pushing them there in the first place," he said. "We decided to put water in the desert, and to organize to change the policies of the INS and Border Patrol."

They chose the symbol of the Big Dipper, drawing the parallel with African-American slaves trying to find their way to freedom, and filled the dipper with water.

The group got permission to place their first two tanks in the Organ Pipe National Monument in March 2001, thanks to the support of two park rangers, Bill Wellman and Dale Thompson, whom Hoover calls "angels."

That spring Humane Borders, based out of the First

Christian Church in Tucson where Hoover is the pastor, was petitioning the Cabeza Prieta National Wildlife Refuge to place tanks there. In April permission was denied. Then on May 23, 14 bodies were found less than a mile from the proposed site of the tanks. The dead were part of a group of 26 migrants who had been trekking through the desert for three days without water. A $42 million wrongful death lawsuit filed by the victims' families against the U.S. Department of the Interior is still pending in federal court.[121] That incident catapulted the border deaths issue, and Humane Borders, into the national media spotlight, and the project took off.

"It exploded like a bag of popcorn," Hoover said.

Now there are tanks in 44 locations in Cochise, Pima, Tucson and Yuma counties. The interfaith organization boasts over 30 member groups, and Hoover and his wife Sue, who quit her job as an administrator at the University of Arizona to help run Humane Borders, are assisted by an army of volunteers ranging from high school and college students to senior citizens. At least one group treks out every single day during the summer months to check on and refill the tanks, driving one of the group's three hefty white pickup trucks outfitted with water tanks, a motorized pump and the ever-present Big Dipper logo on the side. Hoover says that since their inception, 250 volunteers have contributed 2,245 hours delivering 2,200 gallons of water.

On a Saturday in September 2003, Mike Wilson drove several volunteers to the Little Wrench and Trico tank sites near the Saguaro National Monument park. Wilson is a member of the Tohono O'odham nation, an Indian reservation which straddles about 75 miles of the U.S.-Mexico border east of Tucson and Nogales. The Trico and Little Wrench tanks sit right next to the mangled barbed wire fence which designates the start of the reservation.

Currently the reservation is the most popular place for immigrants to cross the border, likely because of the relatively low presence of Border Patrol agents there along with the stepped up Border Patrol and vigilante presence at other parts of the border. The Baboquivari Trail, as the corridor running through the reservation is known, is often called a Trail of Death because of the high number of fatalities there. Tribal officials estimate that 1,500 people cross the reservation every day. In the summer of 2002 there were 86 deaths on the reservation, tribal officials reported, and in 2003 there appeared to be just as many or more.[122]

But in disputes which have frequently been played out in the local media, the Tohono O'odham leadership refuse to allow water stations on their land. As a legally sovereign nation they don't want outside interference; they didn't even allow Border Patrol on the reservation until several years ago. In response Hoover has offered to train tribal members to maintain the stations themselves. They also say the water tanks might encourage even more migration. Leaders of the nation say they are desperately overwhelmed by the influx, with the need for police and hospital services created by the immigrants overwhelming their already cash-strapped community. They also lament the fact that tribal youth are being recruited to participate in drug and human smuggling, and that drug use has increased as a result.

"When they're offering money some youth will get caught up in that," said Wilson, who is both a pastor, special education teacher in training and 21-year veteran of the U.S. military in the Special Forces. He grew up in Ajo, a defunct copper mining town not far from the reservation.

Since Humane Borders is barred from the reservation, Wilson has taken to carrying out his own water operation. Several times a week he gets up before 5 a.m. to drive his own pickup truck as near as possible to the seven sites he maintains, then he uses a wheel barrow to haul multiple one-gallon jugs of water to the sites. The goal is for immigrants to take the jugs with them, and he gets new ones donated from church members. During the summer he finds that people usually take 70 to 80 gallons a week. He noted that in mid-September 2003 he went with a young woman from the reservation to look at the spot where she had just found a migrant's body. The young man died just three miles from one of Wilson's water stations.

"The body was found at mile 24, and I have stations at mile 20 and mile 27," he said.

On this day in September 2003, when the heat has climbed to the high 90s before 10 a.m., the tanks at Little Wrench, sitting below the seemingly watchful eye of a thick saguaro cactus, are still full. But at Trico, a dusty drive off-road under a row of power lines, the three tanks are about half empty. Near them a gray van seat sits primly below a cholla cactus. Wilson notes that finding car and van seats in the area is common, since the smugglers who pick up migrants often tear them out of vehicles to make room to jam in more people.

Along with filling up the water tanks, the Humane Borders volunteers pick up trash left by the migrants, including countless empty water bottles, food wrappers, discarded clothes and other personal items. Hoover maintains a display of some of these items in clear plastic cubes: a package of Boots Mexican cigarettes, La India brand canned meat, a can opener, a baby's shoe, an empty bottle of Jimador tequila, a kerosene lantern with "Antony" written on it. The display has a chilling effect, evoking the physical and mental states of the immigrants as they used and discarded these items and their ultimate fates.

Over the summer Wilson found an especially disturbing item on the reservation—a forked stick with the top meticulously bound in terrycloth, shoe laces and other fabric to make a crutch, presumably for someone who injured their ankle or leg in the crossing.

"That's desperation," he said sadly.

The display serve as part of the public relations campaign that has helped Humane Borders bring the issue of migrant deaths and immigration policy problems to a national audience.

Hoover has been featured in almost every major national media outlet, including an appearance on the Phil Donahue Show where he debated American Border Patrol head Glenn Spencer. He says that overall, public support for the program, both locally and nationally, has been high. But they do have their critics, mostly among the anti-immigrant crowd. A number of the water stations have been vandalized; one in Cochise County, where CHD operates, had to be discontinued because it was vandalized so many times. And even worse, state legislators are discussing a proposed ballot initiative that would end county and state funding to organizations giving aid to undocumented immigrants. If passed, this would cut off the $25,000 a year the group receives from Pima County.[123]

There are several other immigrants' rights and humanitarian groups working along this stretch of the border. Humane Borders shares its gathering spot in the parking lot of the First Christian Church with the group Samaritan Patrol, which was formed in July 2002 by nine faith communities. The Samaritans do regular patrols of the desert looking for migrants in need, and provide them with food, water, first aid, blankets and other supplies. The group BorderLinks and the American Friends Service Committee also operate in the area.

July 2003 was the deadliest month on record for immigrants crossing through Arizona, with at least 50 deaths. Earlier the Border Patrol started an operation aimed at saving lives, called Operation Safeguard. The operation includes the use of 20 rescue beacons with call buttons for agents, two helicopters and 150 additional agents trained in rescue and first aid. Border Patrol statistics showed that as of late July 2003 the effort had likely contributed to  an estimated 3 percent decrease in numbers of people trying to cross, but deaths were up nonetheless.[124]

In September 2003 the Border Patrol in Arizona implemented a policy that could have devastating effects for many immigrants—instead of deporting them back across the Arizona border, about 150 a day are being bused or flown to four cities in Texas—McAllen, El Paso, Del Rio and Laredo—to be deported.[125] The Border Patrol says this is part of their campaign to save lives, by preventing them from trying again to cross the deadly Arizona desert. But immigrants' rights advocates describe it as a travesty, dumping immigrants in totally unfamiliar border cities which are not at all equipped to deal with the influx of homeless immigrants. This is especially a concern in Ciudad Juarez, across the border from El Paso, which is notorious for its violence and the murders, rapes and mutilations of hundreds of young women.

This new policy was also carried out with no advance notice given to the mayors of the affected towns, who have expressed outrage and said their cities are unequipped to deal with the situation.

Garcia notes that immigrants' rights advocates are also embroiled in a fight to prevent the Border Patrol and Department of Homeland Security from building a wall, in some places two walls, that combined with the existing wall in the western part of the state would effectively seal off most of the state's Mexican border. In October 2002 the Border Patrol released a proposal for over 200 miles of fences, roads and 24 hour stadium lights along the border.[126]

A coalition called Bring Down the Wall formed to fight it, and the Border Patrol backed off the plan after getting thousands of letters in opposition. Border Patrol facilities director Jim Caffrey told the Tucson Citizen that the agency got "a little carried away" with the plan, and said it was more infrastructure than the state would need even in case of a war with Mexico.[127]

While immediate plans for the wall have been shelved, Garcia is afraid the government will end up constructing it "piecemeal, like they always do, so people aren't aware of what they're doing until it's too late."

Garcia says that looking at the walls along the border in other parts of Arizona, she gets a sensation which mirrors the one Simcox and his friends are playing out with their camouflage gear, sidearms and walkie talkies.

"We should be grateful to the Mexican people," she said. "But you stand next to this wall, and there's no other feeling you get except we're at war."

For more information:

Derechos Humanos, www.derechoshumanosaz.net.

Humane Borders, www.humaneborders.org.

*Part III*

# THE UNITED STATES

A mural at the Coalition of Immokalee Workers shows the Statue of Liberty as a tomato picker. Photo by Kari Lydersen.

Snapshots of life in the U.S. for Latin Americans create a collage full of color and contradictions.

There are the happy pictures of families in small towns from New Jersey to Nebraska to Nevada, buying their first homes, shopping at Mexican grocery stores in quaint downtowns and earning decent wages at slaughterhouses or construction sites.

Then there are the men and women living under 24-hour armed guard in rural Florida or New Jersey or South Carolina, being forced to work as tomato pickers or prostitutes, and being beaten or even killed for trying to escape.[128]

There are parents grinning in pride as they watch their kids graduate from high school in the U.S., and parents weeping in despair because they haven't seen their kids back in Mexico in five years. Or even worse, because they are being deported back to Mexico and their kids, who are citizens, are staying here.

There is the dejected face of Mercedes Santiago-Felipe, an indigenous Guatemalan woman living in Grand Island, Nebraska whose children were taken away from her and sent to live with white foster parents after a teacher reported Mercedes had slapped her son.[129]

And there is the laughing face of Neris Gonzalez, a Salvadoran woman who survived torture during the civil war there, gained asylum in the U.S. and was able to start an urban gardening program and be reunited with her daughter in Chicago.

Life has never been easy for immigrants in the U.S., especially for undocumented immigrants who are especially vulnerable to being exploited and abused by employers and society at large. It is hard enough for the Latin American immigrants who speak Spanish, not to mention the growing population of indigenous immigrants from southern Mexico and Central and South America who speak only their indigenous languages.

After surviving the arduous trip up to and across the U.S.-Mexico border, many finally arrive in a U.S. city or town to find it is not at all what they expected; the melting pot land of milk and honey is as mythical as a unicorn and their everyday reality involves loneliness, hunger, fatigue and cold.

But it would be a generalization to say there is no opportunity in the U.S. Many do end up forging satisfying new lives here, forming tight-knit communities, going to school, bringing their families to join them and sending enough money back home to create better lives for their relatives there.

For example, the immigrants working in slaughterhouses in Schuyler, Neb. or Beardstown, Ill., who despite the hard and gruesome work are able to save money, buy homes and fund the building of churches and community centers in their hometowns.

Almost everyone agrees that the Sept. 11 attacks turned life upside down for Latin American immigrants in the U.S.

While Arab immigrants and Arab Americans have born the brunt of government surveillance and public suspicion in the wake of the attacks, Latin Americans have also felt the heat. Many Latin Americans can be mistaken for Arab, so they have literally been the target of racial profiling and hate speech from people who blame a whole region of the globe for the attacks on the Twin Towers.

And as noted in the previous section, the Sept. 11-related beefing up of the border has had significant ripple effects for immigrants throughout the U.S., making it harder for family members to reunite or visit each other and increasing the pressure from Border Patrol agents and police. Previously police officers were prohibited from carrying out immigration functions or even demanding to see a green card. But they will actually be required to do so under new national security policies making their way through Congress in early 2004, against the protests of many already-overworked police departments. In San Diego, immigrants and advocates working with the American Friends Service Committee note that brutality and abuses by both Border Patrol and police officers have increased noticeably since Sept. 11, and immigrants live in constant fear of deportation.

On Nov. 14, 2003, for example, a simple trip to J.C. Penney's to return a pair of pants ended in two San Diego area residents getting deported. Police came to the store because a manager had reported an earlier attempted shoplifting by two Mexican men. They questioned the family of Antonio Flores Noyola, even though they had come in after the alleged shoplifting incident, and called the Border Patrol to pick up two of the women who didn't have documents.[130]

This incident was discussed around the country as an example of racial profiling of immigrants. Meanwhile racial profiling has also been charged in the firing and deportations of hundreds of undocumented workers after  workplace sweeps at airports, tourist destinations and other institutions around the country under the mantle of national security.

On December 10, 2002 undocumented workers at Chicago's O'Hare International Airport were systematically fired, along with citizen workers with even minor criminal convictions, as part of a national initiative called Operation Tarmac. Many were placed in deportation proceedings.

Some who hadn't shown up for work that day were arrested in their homes, roughly handled and handcuffed in front of their children. One of the immigrants slated for deportation was Elvira Arellano-Olayo, a Mexican single mother who was working at the airport to support her four-year-old U.S.-born son. Almost a year later, her deportation order was lifted because of intervention by local politicians.[131]

Like all of the other arrestees from the airport sweep, Arellano-Olayo had no links to terrorism. One of the explanations given by government authorities was that while none of the workers were actually suspected of terrorist or criminal activity, the fact that their identities weren't clearly known made them a liability. In all thousands of non-citizen and undocumented workers around the country lost their jobs at airports as a result of the crackdown—for example Latin American as well as a high number of Filipino immigrants were fired at San Francisco's airport, where a whopping 80 percent of the airport's 915 screeners were not citizens.[132]

The increased enforcement of immigration policies post-Sept. 11 has been coinciding with the government's plodding implementation of the draconian 1996 immigration reform laws known as IIRIRA (the Illegal Immigration Reform and Immigrant Responsibility Act). Among other things, this package of laws instituted three to 10 year bars on an immigrant re-entering the country after having been deported, and made violating these bars an offense carrying a jail term.

IIRIRA also expanded the list of crimes for which even legal residents can be deported, to include not only felonies but also drug, gang, or sex-related misdemeanors.

Under the harsh and arbitrary enforcement of IIRIRA just taking effect now, immigrants who thought they were here completely legally are finding themselves in deportation proceedings because they unknowingly missed an appointment with the INS years ago or were convicted of minor marijuana possession or drunk driving charges.

For example Roger Calero, a New York-based journalist who immigrated to the U.S. from Nicaragua as a teenager in 1985, has had legal permanent residency since 1990. But upon returning from a trip to Mexico in December 2002, he found himself arrested because of a 1988 charge for marijuana possession, which he had willingly revealed on his original green card application. His deportation order was eventually reversed thanks to lobbying from his fellow journalists and labor union leaders, but the others he spent time with in a Houston immigration detention center weren't so lucky. He noted that one elderly man in the detention center had actually helped build the center as an undocumented laborer decades ago.

"These are people with kids, houses, the whole successful American dream and now they're getting deported," Calero said. "These are the big 'terrorists' and 'criminals' our country is worried about."

Another devastating occurrence for undocumented immigrants over the last few years has been the wave of Social Security administration "No Match" letters sent out to thousands of employers. Theoretically, the letters are only meant to notify employers that their employees' reported Social Security numbers don't match federal records for disbursing funds. In many cases employers fire the workers upon getting the letters, usually out of genuine fear of legal trouble or in some cases as an excuse to get rid of employees who are agitating for better working conditions or union representation.[133]

"The impetus for the letters being sent was that Congress wanted to collect the $4 billion that was being held suspended in the social security accounts," noted Diego Bonesatti, an organizer at the Illinois Coalition for Immigrant and Refugee Rights. "Then when a worker is fired after getting a no-match letter, they lose all their seniority and have to start over somewhere else at the bottom. So it has the effect of keeping labor costs low."

The No Match letters picked up steam around the same time as the Supreme Court's April 2002 Hoffman decision (Hoffman Plastic Compounds vs. the National Labor Relations Board), a devastating blow to immigrant workers' rights. Essentially, the decision gutted undocumented workers' right to organize a union, by mandating that if an undocumented worker is illegally fired for organizing activities, he cannot sue for back wages.[134]

Immigrants rights groups railed against the Hoffman decision and launched informational campaigns regarding the No Match letters, contacting employers to assure them that the No Match letters aren't grounds for firing a worker.

These campaigns are an example of the slow and unglamorous but often effective and very necessary work that immigrants' rights groups are doing around the country. Another example of day to day organizing that has a concrete effect on immigrants' lives is the workers center movement, wherein immigrant laborers are organizing their own hiring halls complete with popular education and legal aid components to subvert the highly exploitative and fly-by-night temporary labor contracting industry.

The effort to organize a workers center in the Albany Park neighborhood in Chicago is one example of this movement. While the struggle has not gone smoothly—city officials deceived the workers and bulldozed their workers center while some workers fought amongst themselves—it is nonetheless a hopeful example of truly grassroots organizing and cooperation.

Tom Hansen, the director of the Mexico Solidarity Network in Chicago and one of the people involved in supporting the workers center, notes that the increased border security since Sept. 11 may have a small silver lining as it relates to worker organizing drives like the one in Albany Park.

"Undocumented workers have never really had political organizing spaces in the U.S., largely because they are seasonal and temporary workers," said Hansen, who is working on a thesis on the political spaces of Mexican immigrants at the UAM university in Mexico City. "Up until recently they didn't even have a desire to establish political spaces, because their goal was to get home as quickly as possible. But since Sept. 11, the border security has been stepped up so it is harder for people to go home, and a critical mass of Mexicans have arrived in the U.S. allowing social structures to develop and allowing immigrants to really put down roots. So the level of organizing has increased."

While long-term and location-based political spaces and movements may have been rare among Latino immigrants in the past, there is a long history of activism particularly in the agricultural sector, where undocumented immigrants make up one of the country's most abused and low-paid workforces.

Decades after the famous grape boycotts and other organizing drives led by Cesar Chavez, Dolores Huerta and their contemporaries, immigrant farm workers still do backbreaking work for miniscule wages while being exposed to toxic pesticides and paying exorbitant prices for substandard housing.

But the Coalition of Immokalee Workers in southern Florida is among the groups fighting to change that—and succeeding. The Coalition has already gained national attention for its work in combating human slavery and its campaign against Taco Bell, an innovative strategy aimed at holding fast food companies responsible for the conditions in which their raw materials are produced.

Perhaps a similar strategy is needed for other huge companies that employ undocumented immigrants through contractors, places like Wal-Mart, where on Oct. 23, 2003, 250 undocumented immigrant janitors employed by middlemen to clean the stores were arrested. The arrestees included 90 Mexicans and 20 Brazilians along with Eastern Europeans and Mongolians. The immigrants reported working months or even years without a day off, making about $400 per week for 56 to 60 hour weeks.[135]

In the meatpacking industry, some workplaces are unionized and immigrant workers like those in Beardstown, Ill. and Schuyler and Omaha, Neb. are generally paid relatively high wages of $10 or more an hour. But labor abuses and unsafe conditions are still common. The group Amnesty Now describes worker exploitation and labor abuses at Smithfield Foods meatpacking plant in North Carolina, a state where the Latino population has increased from only about 76,000 in 1990 to almost half a million today.[136]

"Their immigration status, coupled with a lack of English language skills and ignorance of their rights, renders them particularly vulnerable to intimidation and exploitation," writes Kristal Brent Zook. "They face high injury rates, lack of job security, and manipulation by union-busting employers." The report tells of a woman from Chiapas working 50 hours a week "in a 35 degree room with blood slicking the floor and animal parts coming at her at the rate of one every 17 seconds."[137]

In January 2003 President Bush announced a new guest worker program in which immigrants living abroad can petition for temporary visas to work for a specific employer. While Mexican President Vicente Fox and some U.S. immigrants' advocacy groups applauded the decision, many U.S. immigrants' groups have denounced the program, seeing it as just a way to institutionalize the availability of cheap and vulnerable immigrant labor. They noted its similarity to the Bracero program instituted in the 1940s, in which labor abuses were rampant and many braceros were never paid their due wages.

"Why, when there are nine million workers—U.S.-born and immigrant alike—unemployed in this country today, do U.S. industries need to look to guest workers to fill their jobs?" said a statement from the Coalition of Immokalee Workers about the program. "For several years, dozens of industries, from meatpacking to fast-food, have complained of labor shortages, while stubbornly offering sub-poverty wages and little or no benefits to potential new hires. Yet rather than raise wages and improve conditions to attract and maintain a stable workforce, as the market would have it, these employers have lobbied their friends in the Bush Administration for the right to circumvent the U.S. labor market altogether and import low-wage workers directly from countries far poorer than the United States. The President's proposal would grant their wish, while cloaking this thinly-veiled subsidy to low-wage industry in the compassionate clothing of immigration reform."

Aside from their battles for legal status and human, civil and labor rights, immigrants living in the U.S. are faced with personal and cultural contradictions and paradoxes on a daily basis. To what extent do they assimilate, thus gaining more economic and social opportunity in the U.S., and to what extent do they preserve and cherish their native culture?

How do immigrant parents feel when their children grow

up more at home in New York or Los Angeles than Mexico City or San Salvador? When these children, listening to hip hop and wearing Tommy Hilfiger, seem embarrassed by their non-English-speaking, conservative-dressing parents? When, even worse, they seem to squander all the risks their parents took to bring them here by joining gangs and dropping out of school? Immigrant parents are often forced to deal with the dualities of pride in their children's assimilation into U.S. culture, and anxiety over the emotional and physical dangers this assimilation poses.

Unfortunately many immigrant youth do turn to gangs for companionship and protection in U.S. cities. Many immigrant youth also end up joining the military, for lack of better economic options or in a surge of patriotism for their new country. Especially in current times, this can be as deadly a choice as the "vida loca" (crazy life) of drugs and gangs.

In fact Mexican immigrants have played a significant role in U.S. military campaigns throughout the past century. In Moline, Ill. there is a street known as Hero Street which supplied the U.S. military with 100 men from 25 families, most of them from Mexican immigrant families. A monument along the street pays homage to the eight residents who were killed in combat in World War II and Korea.

"All were proud of serving their country, but frustrated with discrimination and lack of recognition for their deeds," noted The Moline Dispatch.[138] "Some of the veterans tried to join the local VFW, but were rejected because they were Hispanic."

Many people point out the irony of immigrants dying to defend a country that claims not to want them in the first place. During the 2003 invasion of Iraq, about 37,000 non-citizen immigrants were serving in the military.[139] Yet only after they were killed were some of them awarded U.S. citizenship. Posthumous citizenship was given to one of the first casualties of the Iraq war, Jose Gutierrez, a Guatemalan immigrant who had come to the U.S. illegally as a teenager.[140] While the media praised Gutierrez as a patriot and hero, critics note that the thousands of immigrants serving in the military who haven't yet died deserve the same consideration. As non-citizens not only do they not enjoy the same civil rights as citizens, but they are confined to the lower and more dangerous jobs within the military.

Latinos are especially likely to be in high risk combat positions, making up about 9.5 percent of active-duty personnel but 17.7 percent of the personnel who most directly handle weapons.[141]

Colombian community organizer Norman Ospina doesn't mince words on this topic. One of his campaigns has been to protest and counter ROTC recruitment at Farragut, a largely Latino high school in Chicago.

"We bust our asses here and you use our kids as cannon fodder and all you give us is medals," he said. "It's the ultimate irony. Salvadorans are forced out of their country by U.S. intervention, then for lack of other opportunities they join the military in the U.S. and end up killing people in Iraq or Colombia or Venezuela."

Many activist immigrants note that it is a constant challenge to balance striving for a better life and specific political victories here in the U.S. while not losing sight of the larger struggle for social and economic justice around the world. Ospina notes that this is something he thinks about constantly during all his campaigns, whether it's getting undocumented immigrants access to food stamps or in-state college tuition or drivers licenses. He pointed out that the restoration of food stamps for immigrants, which had been cut in 1996, was attached to a bill for U.S. farm subsidies, which combined with NAFTA are a major cause of economic devastation in Mexico.

"So immigrants will get their food stamps back but how many thousands more will have to migrate to the U.S. because they can't compete with subsidized U.S. corn?" he asked. "Do we want our students to go to college just so they can work for a corporation and come back and exploit other people? Do we want licenses so we can drive Lincoln Esplanades? It's not just about licenses or the student adjustment act, it's about social change and economic change on a systemic international level."

# CHAPTER ELEVEN

# Picking Mushrooms and Killing Cows

## Immigration in Small Town Illinois

### DePue: The Mushroom Beds

Norteño music blares through the dark, dripping rooms where workers straddle stacked beds of manure piled eight feet high, carefully picking the mature mushrooms from among the plentitude of round white caps sprouting in the musty black material.

Among the names scrawled on each stack of beds are Gustavo, Aidee, Efrain, Ramos. Signs reminding workers to wash their hands are printed in English, Spanish and Laotian.

The workers at the Monterey Mushrooms plant in the tiny town of DePue, Ill. are predominantly Mexican. They operate forklifts in a vast warehouse of steaming piles of manure; man assembly lines where mushrooms are sliced, diced, sorted and shrink-wrapped with mind-boggling speed; drive little trains pulling stacks of mushroom-filled cartons through damp, dark hallways; and pile packaged mushrooms in 35-degree cooling rooms.

In the special section for portabella mushrooms, many of the workers are also Laotian women.

This is a glimpse of the modern face of much of the farming industry, and of immigration, in the American Midwest.

With the wide-scale automation of farming practices, from plowing and seeding to packaging, the need for manual labor in the industry has significantly decreased. But there are some jobs that will probably never become automated, like straddling the stacks of mushroom beds to select the mature mushrooms in groups of three and snipping their stems off, while leaving the non-mature caps intact.

Whether it is mushroom farming, apple picking or de-tassling corn, these remaining non-automated farming jobs are the hardest of the hard, entailing long hours of intense physical labor in less than comfortable environments, like the stinking manure warehouse or the freezing storage rooms. Not surprisingly, the majority of white people and other American citizens don't want these jobs. So they are left for immigrants, many of them undocumented and fleeing dire economic and political situations in Latin America, Africa or Asia.

"Anything mechanized is still done by Anglos, while anything that cannot be mechanized is done by immigrants," said Louise Cainkar, formerly a researcher with the Illinois Coalition for Immigrant and Refugee Rights (ICIRR). "Corn harvesting is still done by Anglos, because that's a mechanized process. But immigrants are de-tassling, the part of production that still has to be done manually. The manual aspects of agriculture and meat processing are done mostly by immigrants."

There are only about 1,600 people in DePue, which is known mainly for its yearly speedboat races. Monterey Mushrooms employs about 500 people, from DePue as well as surrounding small towns including LaSalle, Peru and Ottawa. About three quarters of the Monterey workers are Mexican, according to workers and supervisors.

"There are only two American [Anglo] women in harvesting, the same number as when I first started here," said Delores Cain, the harvesting supervisor, who has been at the factory for more than 20 years.

"The work is too hard for them [Anglos]," added Alfredo Godizes, another harvesting supervisor.

The Monterey plant sells about 400,000 pounds of mushrooms each week to clients like Jewel, Domino's Pizza and even the U.S. Army. It is not unionized, but pay is relatively good. The pickers work piecemeal, which most say they like, and earn an average of $10 an hour working seven to 12 hour days. Pay is about $9 an hour for packing, wharf and assembly line jobs, according to human resources manager Michelle Rispoli.

The plant is essentially the lifeblood of the town, supporting a small but vital community that includes two Mexican grocery stores, a Catholic church with masses in Spanish, a tiny public library and a few bars in the downtown. There is a section of the town called "White City" which was formerly home to white residents and now houses many Mexicans. The name refers not to race but to the fine white dust that settles on cars from the nearby factories.

Heavy industry as well as farming is part of the local fabric in DePue, as in many small towns. That means that immigrants in these rural areas, like immigrants in the poorer areas of major cities, suffer the de facto effects of environmental racism. They say the once-clear lake is contaminated by silt and pollution from steel plants and factories in the area. The nearby zinc smelting plant was shut down by the government for environmental violations, and residents report remediation has still not been completed on the heaps of slag that sit next to the town.

Last year Monterey had about 40 percent turnover because of workers moving to the newly built Wal-Mart regional distribution center for jobs. As with Monterey, many people in Mexico heard about jobs at Wal-Mart and migrated north specifically for that reason.

"It's all word of mouth," said Cainkar. "They're coming here to work and raise money for their families, so they come when they hear about jobs."

In many small towns like DePue, the population of Latinos has increased many-fold in the past decade as immigrants and refugees have come for farm work like the mushroom factory. The number of people from the Middle East, Asia and Africa who have moved into small midwestern towns has also risen significantly. In Illinois the Latino population grew 34.6 percent and the Asian population by 36.4 percent between 1990 and

1998. In Iowa, the Latino population grew a whopping 73.5 percent. The Latino population of Ohio has increased 27.5 percent between 1990 and 1998, while the Asian population increased 38 percent.[142] While some of this increase is in major cities like Chicago and Cleveland, a large percent of the increase is in small farming towns like DePue.

"In the last 10 years there's been a major increase in immigration to the U.S. in general and also parallel to that a major shift to areas away from the big cities," said Cainkar. "They're going to areas like Iowa and Nebraska where a lot of immigrants didn't used to go."

In tiny Arcola, Ill., Latino immigrants are employed making the town's famous Amish brooms. In Joslin, Ill. hundreds of Latino immigrants as well as Bosnian and African refugees work at a meatpacking plant. In southern Illinois many immigrants come to pick apples, and in central Illinois immigrants work in corn mills and other types of farming or food processing.

This quick growth has led to growing pains and racial tensions in some areas, as well as cultural fusion.

"It can be hard, there's some tension, you hear comments like 'What are you bringing these people in for?'" said Ann Grove, director of the Moline, Ill. Office of World Relief, which helps resettle refugees from Africa and other countries. "But most people are supportive, and employers are amazed at their work ethic."

On a summer afternoon in 2002 a group of Latinos gathered in a lakefront park in DePue, which was once a port of entry for immigrants including Slovenians, Italians and Irish, to talk about some tensions with residents of European descent.

"When my mother and father first got here, it was difficult," said Felisitas Garetto, 68, whose parents came to the U.S. from a small town in Jalisco, Mexico called Lagos de Moreno. "They didn't want Hispanics here. But it doesn't make sense for them to look down on us because they were from somewhere else also. It's not like they were native born from DePue."

## Beardstown: The Slaughterhouse

Father Tomas Alvarez is a man constantly in motion at the site of his new Church of the Nazarene in the small town of Beardstown, Ill.

One minute he is showing visitors the brightly painted rooms and airy sanctuary that are being built in the former trucking depot. Then he is joking with Larry Cline, a Beardstown native who did construction work in Washington D.C. and Saudi Arabia before returning here and helping to build the church.

They are interrupted by a steady stream of visitors—an older Spanish-speaking woman whose disability benefits have been denied, a young Mexican man who received a letter telling him his services wouldn't be needed at the Excel Pork Processing Plant just a mile or so from the church.

Alvarez offers to help them all.

In addition to preaching the gospel, he guides his 100 or so parishioners through dealings with the INS and their employers; teaches English as a Second Language classes; runs a nursery; and even copy-edits the one-year-old Spanish language newspaper, *La Estrella.*

Alvarez and his wife and four children came to Beardstown from Guadalajara, Mexico four years ago. They are part of a Mexican migration to the formerly German town that has given Cass County the state's biggest jump in foreign-born population between the 1990 and 2000 censuses.[143]

And as in other parts of the country, social service providers in Beardstown note that Mexican immigrants, especially undocumented ones, were grossly undercounted in the census. They say the town of about 12,000 has 2,500 to 3,000 Latino residents, most of them from Mexico as well as growing populations from Central America.

This means that where once "no one even knew what a Hispanic person was," in one resident's words, now there are whole sections of town that look just like pueblos in Mexico.

In Beardstown, the majority of Latino immigrants come for one reason: to work at the Excel slaughterhouse, where 17,000 hogs a day go through the killing line.

At Excel, starting workers make $10.05 an hour with benefits, and the company has made it known that if workers come, there will be jobs for them. So the word has spread in Mexico and throughout Mexican communities in Texas, California, Arizona and other parts of the U.S.

The Excel plant, which now employs about 2,000 workers, opened in 1987 shortly after the closing of an Oscar Mayer slaughterhouse and the town's other major employer, Bohn Aluminum. Longtime residents note that as Excel expanded and local white residents went looking for more pleasant work, the company started recruiting in Latino communities.

Waves of Latinos, both documented and undocumented, started coming in 1996 and haven't stopped.

"Before it was a revolving door, people would come for a while and then leave," said Alvarez. "Now people are buying houses and staying. The Mexicans like it here. They can buy a house and a car, things that are really difficult to get in Mexico. Some were working 12-hour days in the fields in California, so they like that they can come here and work inside, earn $10.05 and only work eight hours. And they all send money back to Mexico."

Like in DePue, in the early days of the migration there were problems with racial tensions and cultural misunderstandings.

"It went from like nothing to about 1,000 [immigrants] overnight, and the community wasn't ready," said Mary Ellen Murphy, a staff member at the Cass County Mental Health Services office in Beardstown.

It didn't help when a Latino man shot and killed a white man at a bar called El Flamingo in 1996. Jorge Arambula avoided an arrest warrant by fleeing to Mexico, and the country refused to extradite him. The day after the murder a cross was burned outside the bar, prompting the FBI to open a civil rights probe.[144]

"Things were very tense then," said Missie Young, a Beardstown native and editor at the *Cass County Star-Gazette*. "Things have improved a lot now. It's more of a live and let live situation. There's some interaction but it's kind of like two different towns."

Today the elementary and high schools offer bilingual classes, there are several Mexican restaurants and grocery stores and even the American grocery stores have Mexican sections. There is reportedly some racial tension among small groups of high school students—an impending whites versus Latinos brawl is rumored and a park bench overlooking the river sports anti-Mexican graffiti and a swastika.

"We're hearing that kids are carrying knives in the high school, some of them have shaved their heads, some have a swastika shaved in the back of their heads," said Murphy. "But it's really just a small group of wannabes that are taunting each other."

Residents report that some landlords also charge Mexicans significantly higher rents than whites. And they say that the largely white police force tends to harass or racially profile Latino residents, resulting in a pending class action lawsuit.

But overall white and Latino residents say the two cultures are getting along well together.

"We're moving toward being a more open-minded, culturally open town," said Cline, 51, as he tied wire around steel rebar to lay a foundation for a vestibule of the church. "People aren't as prejudiced as they used to be and especially the kids in school are molding together. I think that any time you have a multinational community you grow and thrive."

For more information: The Illinois Coalition for Immigrant and Refugee Rights, www.icirr.org.

A mural in Chicano Park, downtown San Diego celebrates activist Patricia Marin. Photo by Pat Lydersen.

Chicano Park was built after a struggle between local Latinos and the city government in San Diego. Photo by Pat Lydersen.

# CHAPTER TWELVE

# In the Shadows of "America's Finest City"

## The Ripple Effects of Sept. 11 in San Diego

Since Sept. 11, Anna says she has been living in a state of terror.

But it's not Al Qaeda the 34-year-old mother of two living in San Diego is afraid of. It's the police and la migra (immigration officials).

She refuses to take the public trolley, for fear immigration officials will make one of their periodic raids while she is on it. She's afraid to go to the laundromat or the grocery stores in the Latino area of town, also frequent targets of immigration raids.

"We're afraid to leave the house at all," said Anna, not her real name, during a June 2003 interview at the American Friends Service Committee (AFSC) office in the largely-Latino Grant Hill neighborhood in San Diego. "We're afraid we'll walk out the door and never come back. Because of the Border Patrol, we can't live in peace and dignity. We live with many types of fear, daily. It's not temporary, it's every day."

She's even terrified to drive her car, since as an undocumented immigrant she can't legally get a driver's license and the police could stop her for some minor infraction and arrest her for driving without a license at any time.

In fact she was previously stopped by the police for driving without a license, and while she was lucky enough not to get deported, her car was impounded and this fee along with various other minor charges they slapped her with added up to about $900—several weeks' wages.

In states around the country, immigrants' groups are carrying out campaigns to win the right for undocumented people to have drivers' licenses. But it can be an uphill battle politically. California governor Arnold Schwarzenegger made preventing undocumented immigrants from getting drivers licenses a major tenet of his campaign, even though he is an immigrant himself. One of his first actions after taking office was to repeal a measure that would have allowed two million undocumented immigrants in the state to apply for licenses.

Anna is wracked by stabs of fear every time she sees a Border Patrol van, which means almost every day in San Diego.

Even worse than her own fear, she's afraid of what her 11-year-old daughter is going through, afraid of the lifelong scars her daughter will bear from experiencing discrimination and hatred at such a young age. From being made to feel like a criminal just because she is an undocumented immigrant.

Anna starts to cry as she describes how she took her daughter to Wal-Mart one day recently, only to see a Border Patrol van near the entrance. She tried to turn back to the car without her daughter seeing, making some excuse about forgetting something at home, but it was too late. Her daughter knew exactly what the green and white van meant. "She said, 'It's better they take me than you, because you need to stay here for [her son],'" said Anna.

Anna explains how she and her daughter have a plan if they are ever picked up by the Border Patrol. The daughter is supposed to give the name of her cousin, who is a legal resident.

"That's teaching her how to think like a criminal, how to hide her own identity," said Anna. "A little girl shouldn't be made to feel like a criminal. What does that do to her psychologically and emotionally? As a mother I'm supposed to protect her psychological health, but these are realities that I can't change."

Anna didn't ask for this life. She didn't want to leave her

country in the first place.

"I cried and cried about leaving my homeland and my people," she said.

But like thousands of others, Anna had no choice but to leave her home, in Guadalajara, Mexico. Her husband was an alcoholic, and his addiction led to them losing their home and most of their belongings. Anna had no way to support herself and her young daughter. But she had family in the U.S., so like so many others throughout Latin America, 10 years ago she decided to make the treacherous journey through the mountains along the border into the U.S.

Later she sent for her daughter to join her. In the U.S., she had a son, who is now five. She is raising them both as a single mother. Her son, who was born here, is a citizen. Her daughter is not.

"These are both my children, but my son has rights and my daughter doesn't," she said. "It's discrimination."

Every day she and her daughter are reminded of what it means to be a citizen and what it means to be "illegal." The dichotomy is everywhere, especially in a border town like San Diego. The dichotomy is in their own family. Her son can go on field trips to other states with his school class. He can visit their relatives in Washington. He can even visit family in Mexico. At Christmas he gets toys from local charities who serve low-income families. He gets certain medical benefits. Her daughter gets none of this.

The year after she made it to the U.S., her mother became seriously ill. It was a major decision whether to go back to see her or not. She decided to go, meaning she had to risk the treacherous crossing back into the U.S. all over again.

"It's so many mixed emotions," she said. "Of course you want to see your family. But then you have to make decisions, if I get deported, is it worth it? You should never be forced to make that decision."

Anna was able to make it back into the U.S. again after

seeing her mother. Today, she says, it would be a different story.

"Since Operation Gatekeeper, it's almost impossible," she said.

Operation Gatekeeper, the extreme increase in security measures along the Baja-California border, was started in 1994. Before Gatekeeper, the Tijuana-San Diego border was basically marked by only an approximately six-foot-tall corrugated metal fence. Today, there are three fences in some areas. From the ocean to the San Ysidro checkpoint and a bit beyond, there is the original fence plus a new barrier made of tightly spaced concrete pylons topped by a slanting screen. At some parts, a third fence is also in place. Republican politicians have pushed for plans for a third fence spanning the entire area. In addition to the fences, high-powered stadium lights illuminate most of the border along Tijuana, giving it an eerie glow at night. Border patrol cars are also stationed every few hundred yards throughout the dusty hills on either side of the already-heavily secured border.

AFSC organizer Christian Ramirez, a native of San Ysidro, the town directly across the border from Tijuana, notes that the Border Fields State Park adjacent to the beach along the border used to be one of the only places Mexican and U.S. residents could talk face to face—through the chain-link fence which goes into the ocean for about 50 yards at the border. But now the park and beach on the U.S. side are closed most of the time.

"They say it's for environmental reasons or other excuses, but we think it's so people can't see each other there," said Ramirez, noting that the AFSC and other groups used to organize protests and solidarity actions along the fence at the beach.

Since Sept. 11, security at the border has gotten even tighter. The effects of Sept. 11 have also made life in San Diego, as in cities throughout the country, much harder for immigrants. As Anna said, undocumented immigrants are living in terror.

"It is totally different since Sept. 11," she said. "They see us all as terrorists. Immigrants work for a better life, while terrorists destroy things. We're the opposite of terrorists, we're here for peace. But we are suffering discrimination as if we were the terrorists."

In June 2003 she was fired from her $10 an hour job as a clerical worker for a labor union, where she had been working for three years. She says she was fired because she didn't have a valid social security number. As in other parts of the country, hundreds of employees have been fired in different workplaces around San Diego since Sept. 11 for not having valid Social Security numbers.

Now, unemployed and with the prospects for an undocumented worker harder than ever, Anna is unsure what she will do to support her kids.

"I'm looking for any kind of work I could get," she says. "But it's very hard."

As afraid as she is, Anna is determined to fight back. She is one of about 20 members of the Women's Committee Patricia Marin, a group which was formed around 1996 with the goal of empowering undocumented women and addressing the specific challenges and abuses that women face in San Diego, from persecution by immigration officials to domestic violence.

Committee organizer Adriana Jasso noted that the type of fear and oppression that Anna has faced (along with her courage and strength in the face of this) is a common story.

"These women are subject to violence on so many levels," she said. "Mexican working class women really bear the brunt of the violence inherent in the system."

While telling her story at the AFSC office, Anna was surrounded by 177 empty gallon water jugs plastered with the words "Ni Una Mas"—"Not One More." The jugs represent the immigrants who died crossing the border during June, July and August of 2002.

The deaths rose exponentially after Operation Gatekeeper took effect, from a handful each year to hundreds. After four and a half years of Gatekeeper, there had been a total of 389 deaths along this portion of the border.[145] Most died from heat in the desert or cold in the mountains. Others drowned while swimming across the fast-moving, ironically named All-American Canal near Calexico, in the Imperial Valley east of San Diego. Still others swim through the heavily polluted New River in the same area. Word on the street is that Border Patrol agents won't venture near the river because it is so polluted— the migrants who brave it are at risk of catching diseases.

Deaths from exposure and violence used to happen frequently at the San Diego-Tijuana border, in the Tijuana River Valley. Since Operation Gatekeeper, however, only a handful of people try to cross at this border. Deaths and injuries here have gone down significantly, but that is only because migrants have been pushed farther east, into the harsh conditions of the Imperial Valley about a two hour's drive or more to the east. Some immigrants skip Baja altogether, and instead cross the border in the desolate mountains or deserts along Arizona and Texas.

Though deaths at the border near San Diego have largely stopped, violence against immigrants continues.

In front of the gray, nondescript buildings of Southwestern College in San Ysidro, there is a monument made of tarnished, rust-stained white marble blocks. A plaque below the monument lists the names of 21 people who "tragically died" on July 18, 1984.

At that time, the building that now houses the college was a McDonald's. On that day, a Vietnam vet named James Huberty who frequently professed his hatred of Mexicans told his wife he was going "hunting humans." He strolled into the McDonald's with an Uzi and other guns and opened fire.

Ramirez notes that many in the community were unhappy with the marble block monument, because neither it nor the accompanying plaque give a real description of what they say happened on this site on that day in 1984. They feel the white marble and vague language obscure the pure hate and racism that was manifested here.

That hate is what brought Roberto Martinez to where he is today. Martinez, 67, is a sixth-generation Mexican-American.

"In 1831 my great-great-grandfather was born in what is now Texas, before there was a border there," he said. "Then there was also racism, violence, the Indian wars. The things going on in my time are an extension of what was going on then."

When Martinez and his family moved to the town of Santee east of San Diego in the 1960s, they were one of the first Latino families there. Soon others started moving in. Tensions flared in the formerly all-white community, and white teenagers started wearing jackets with white power symbols on them and the words Youth Klan Kore. They would wait after school with baseball bats for the Mexican kids. One day someone called the police, and only the Mexican students ended up getting arrested, and beaten to boot—several students sustained serious injuries from the abuse.

So Martinez became an activist.

Almost 40 years later, he is still fighting.

And almost 40 years later, white teenagers are still beating up Mexicans.

"I'm working with a family now whose son and his friends were attacked by boys from [nearby] El Capitan High School wearing jackets with Nazi symbols on them," he said. "I'd say things are worse than they were before."

He noted that in the summer of 2000, eight teenage boys viciously beat and tortured five elderly Mexican immigrant workers in a campsite in Carmel Valley, near San Diego, while making racial slurs.

Prosecutors in the case said the boys shot the immigrants with pellet guns, hit them with steel rods and rocks, robbed them and tried to burn the makeshift shelters at their encampment. One of the victims was knocked unconscious, dragged into the bushes and left for dead, according to investigators.

However despite the racial slurs the boys weren't even charged with hate crimes, only with charges including elder abuse and robbery.

"On one hand these are random acts of violence, but they know what they're doing," Martinez said. "This is part of a pattern of occurrences. In almost every case they're quoted as saying, 'Let's go hunt some beaners' or something like that. But they aren't classified as hate crimes. The juries and judges don't see these as serious crimes because the victims are undocumented immigrants."

Regular citizens aren't the only ones attacking immigrants in San Diego. Martinez is also heavily involved in a campaign to bring attention to police brutality committed against immigrants. In March 2002, an immigrant with mental problems was shot to death by seven officers while holding "an empty, nonlethal weapon."[146] And the previous summer, two undocumented women were beaten by an officer in the trendy Pacific Beach neighborhood.

"I have been filing complaints for over 30 years and nothing seems to change," said Martinez.

One of Martinez's current crusades is the issue of high-speed, sometimes deadly car chases between Border Patrol agents and coyotes. Even if immigrants cross the border farther east in the Imperial Valley, they still come to San Diego in vehicles with coyotes to stay in safe houses and then start journeys to look for work in other parts of the country. Border Patrol agents are locked in a cat and mouse struggle with these coyotes, determined to catch them at any cost. When officers start pursuing a coyote, most will take off at high speed. To stop the vehicles, authorities will often throw "spike strips" down on the road.[147]

"The smugglers see the strip and swerve, causing them to roll," Martinez said. "That will kill eight or nine people at a time. And these high speed chases don't just endanger Border Patrol and immigrants, they put the innocent American public at risk. We know the smugglers hold some responsibility, but there has to be a better way to deal with this."

In October 2001, two men were killed and about 19 seriously injured after Border Patrol agents started chasing a van driven by smugglers while other agents threw a spike strip on the freeway.

"We do not disagree that the smugglers who drive these vehicles have to share some of the blame for trying to outrun the Border Patrol," says a report by the American Friends Service Committee. "However, chasing vehicles only forces the smugglers to take even more dangerous and evasive action. Why would the Border Patrol throw a spike strip down in front of a smuggler's vehicle that is racing down the freeway at 80 to 90 miles an hour? What do they think is going to happen when the vehicle runs over those spikes?"

Martinez and others are working to set up meetings between Border Patrol agents and the public about high-speed chases and spike strips. He notes that past efforts at demanding more accountability from the Border Patrol have gone nowhere, since the agencies responsible for overseeing the patrol—namely the Department of Justice—are all part of the same system. Extremely high turnover among Border Patrol agents also makes training and enforcement on such seemingly basic things as avoiding lethal chases difficult.

Violence and abuses by police and border patrol are not going unchecked, however. Since joining the women's committee, Anna has picked up some new tools—cameras. Even as "la migra" patrols the area looking for undocumented immigrants, the women from the Patricia Marin committee hold community patrols, turning the lens of public scrutiny back on the authorities. They photograph, videotape and otherwise document abuses by Border Patrol, police and military members. Anna thinks the patrols have had a significant effect.

"It's definitely made a difference," she said. "They have to be more careful around us now. Sometimes I think they're walking on eggshells because they know we're watching them. It's a way for us to take control."

For more information:

The Raza Rights Coalition, PO Box 620095

San Diego, CA 92113/

coalicionproderechos@hotmail.com.

San Diego American Friends Service Committee, www.afsc.org/pacificsw/sandiego.htm

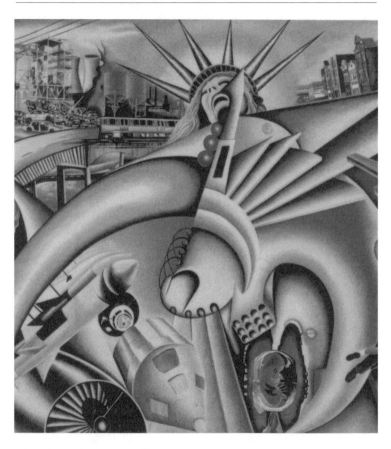

Cataclysm by Marcos Raya.

# CHAPTER THIRTEEN

# Not in My Backyard
## The Albany Park Workers Center

*August 28, 2003*

Almost every morning for eight years, since he came here from his hometown of Tegucigalpa, Honduras, Roberto Zavala has been showing up at a specific spot in the Albany Park neighborhood on Chicago's northwest side to wait for work.

First it was in the parking lot of a McDonald's, then it was a Salvation Army, now it is a vacant plot of land with a semicircular driveway perfect for contractors to drive up and recruit workers. About 60 to 80 men show up here with Zavala every morning; like him many of them have been doing it for years. They come from almost every country in Latin America— Ecuador, Chile, El Salvador, Honduras, Venezuela, Uruguay, Mexico.

There are also workers from Mongolia and Korea, among other countries, and a few natives of the U.S. Many of the immigrants are undocumented, which makes off the books day labor like this one of their only employment options. This group of men loosely consider themselves to be a "workers center," part of a growing national movement to create physical and political spaces for day laborers and other immigrant and low-income workers to co-operate to fight for better pay and conditions.

"The workers center was born out of the necessity to organize," says Zavala, speaking in rapid-fire Spanish with unblinking intensity. "Because of language barriers and immigration status, the immigrants who come to this country can't develop professions. [Day labor] is a necessity in order to bring food to our homes and help our families in our countries. It doesn't matter what country you are from, the doors are open here."

The contractors who drive up will hire them to do construction, gardening, electric wiring, roofing, ceramics or other hard manual labor, at wages ranging roughly from $6 to $20 or more an hour, depending on the work and the workers' level of experience. Some workers say they earn as much as $1,000 a week. Others earn just enough to scrape by.

This is a much better situation than they would find going to one of the temporary day labor agencies with names like Manpower, Trojan and Elite that line the streets of low-income immigrant neighborhoods throughout the country.

At these agencies, horror stories abound. Workers tell of being crammed into unsafe vehicles for transportation to work sites, and charged exorbitantly for the ride. Of being left out at work sites with no idea where they are or how to get home, and never being paid for their work. Even under the best conditions, once transportation and equipment costs are deducted from their paychecks and waiting time is figured in, they often make less than minimum wage going through temp agencies. Gender discrimination and sexual harassment are also rampant in the industry—women have a hard time getting hired for day jobs by the temp agencies, and when they are they are often sexually harassed and sometimes find themselves transported to strip bars or houses of prostitution. While Chicago and other cities and states have passed ordinances regulating the day labor industry, it continues to be a shady, fly-by-night business where workers, especially undocumented ones, are regularly deceived and find their rights hard to enforce.[148]

That's why independent workers centers like the one Zavala helped found are so important. Here there is no middleman to pay, they can set their own terms of employment and they have a venue to do community organizing and popular education.

A national day labor workers center movement has sprung up, with centers in locations ranging from the rural south and the Ozarks to major cities like Los Angeles and Phoenix. The

National Study on Workers Centers, published in May 2003, reports that there are a total of 113 workers centers around the country, With the highest numbers in California (21), New York (20) and Illinois (7).[149] At a 2003 national workers center conference in Chicago, workers advocates from around the country discussed the challenges of easing racial tensions between workers, building truly grassroots centers and negotiating the complexities of immigration and labor law.

The goal in Albany Park has long been to have a workers center with a suitable building that serves as a hiring hall as well as a classroom and organizing locus.

"We want a permanent center where workers can be inside, negotiate their own contract and learn workers rights and English," noted Jose Landaverde, a Salvadoran immigrant who has extensive experience organizing workers centers.

Albany Park is a long-time port of entry for immigrants, with large Greek, Korean, Romanian, Bosnian and Jewish populations along with the Latinos. But the area is quickly gentrifying—it has the most-rapidly-rising property values in the city. And as usually happens in such cases, that means that lower income immigrants are finding it harder to afford their rent as higher-income professionals start to move in.[150] Nonetheless, the area remains home to many of the immigrant workers who are lobbying for the workers center.

At the bus-turnaround site, the workers built a wooden house, or casita, for shade and shelter. Often there is a grill fired up outside.

But the Chicago city government is trying to shut this workers center down. A group of local residents going by the name Neighbors United have been complaining that the men sell drugs, get drunk and harass passersby.

The alderman who represents the area where the center is located, Margaret Laurino, says the plot of land is needed for a bike path. Workers argue that the bike path and the workers center could easily co-exist. They are sure the real reason

Laurino and the neighbors want them out is plain old racism. (Laurino didn't return calls for comment.)

"The reason she doesn't want us here is racism," said Ricardo, a young man from Guanajato, Mexico who has been with the workers center group for six years. "We're good people, humble, we just come here to work, we even pay taxes. We came here for a better life."

Tom Hansen, director of the Mexico Solidarity Network which has its offices just around the corner from the center, also feels the neighbors who want to see the workers moved are motivated by racism.

"They pretend to have the same goals as us, saying they want a center for the workers—somewhere else," he said. "Really they are hardcore racists. They always talk about 'those people.' 'Those people took over my restaurant' [a nearby diner where workers congregate], those people don't pay taxes, those people taught my son to pee in the front yard.'"

The workers faced similar pressure from local residents when they used to congregate outside two other nearby sites, McDonalds and the Salvation Army. After on-and-off battles with the city over the vacant bus turn-around site, on Aug. 26, 2003 police officers raided it and knocked down the wooden shelter. This was done while many of the workers and supportive community activists were at a meeting with city officials at City Hall. They see the timing as no coincidence. They think they were purposely lured away for the meeting so police could knock down the casita with less resistance.

"It was like they knocked down a church, there was even an imagen (religious image) there," said Oscar, an immigrant from Cuenca, Ecuador.

City officials put up signs in English, Spanish and Korean noting that the workers center was being temporarily moved to a K-Mart parking lot a few miles away.

But the workers point out that this is no solution—it takes months to build up a relationship with employers, who know where to go to look for workers. The K-Mart lot is also completely lacking in shade trees and any kind of shelter or area for the workers to comfortably gather.

So despite the fact that police cars are blocking the entrance to the bus turn-around, and they are forced to congregate on the sidewalk, they are determined to stay put.

"We pay taxes, we contribute to the internal development of the city," said Zavala. "We need laws to protect our human rights and workers' rights to be here."

"We are going to fight for this place," added Ricardo. "This place is the best. There aren't problems with traffic, there aren't accidents caused when the contractors stop on the street."

As the day gets hotter a fight almost breaks out between two workers. Some move to intervene, others watch and laugh.

Some of the workers say they feel "like family" to each other. Nonetheless, most of them miss their real families in their home countries badly.

Oscar has a wife and two boys in Ecuador—"macho men," he calls them—age 14 and 16. He is hoping to go back soon to see them, but the astronomical cost to come back to the U.S.—about $12,000—and the uncertainty of getting back in the country mean it is hardly an option.

Two other young men who wait on the sidewalk near Zavala are also from Tegucigalpa, Honduras. Frank, 23, came here a year and a half ago in search of economic opportunity, after first stopping in Dallas. He has brothers here who are legal residents. He supports a wife and four children—two boys and two girls—here in the U.S. and also sends money back to Honduras.

"In our country we're suffering from a bad economy," he said. "There are jobs but they don't pay much."

To reach the U.S.-Mexico border, he spent six days and nights stowed away in a train car, with no food at all and no water for the last few days. He crossed the border in the winter, walking for three days in the desert and discarding his coat even in the freezing weather to be able to move more easily. Finally he reached Chicago traveling by bus.

"We endure a lot of suffering coming here—cold, thirst, hunger," he said. "But they're never going to stop people from entering. One thousand will come, five thousand will come." Franqui Monzon, 33, came here at age 20 from Guatemala fleeing the decades-long civil war.

"We were teenagers at the time, seeing blood all over the place," he said, in English. "There would be blood in the rivers. When we realized we were killing our own brothers, we ran away to this country. But then we found out this country didn't want us, even though they were the ones who supported the war in our country."

He hasn't been back to Guatemala since, though his parents and brothers and sisters still live in a small town near the border with Mexico.

"It's a high price you pay to come here and stay way from your family," he said. "My parents want to see my kids."

Monzon doesn't feel the U.S. owes him anything.

"They don't want us here, and we don't belong here," he said. "I work if they let me, but they're only protecting their own country. I would do the same thing if I was a citizen."

He says he won't mind leaving, in fact he is eager to go back to Guatemala.

"When you go back they think you've fallen from heaven," he said. "When I go back I'll make a big noise, a big scream."

Along with the Albany Park campaign, Landaverde and a group he founded called the Latino Union are fighting to establish workers centers on the grounds of two Home Depots in the Chicago metropolitan area. They argue that Home Depot benefits indirectly from the workers' labor, so it should offer them a center. Already large groups of workers congregate at the Home Depots, but they say they are often arrested or chased away by police in the parking lots.

"They help bring Home Depot a lot of business, because people can get the materials and the workers at the same time," he said.

Landaverde came here as a refugee from the civil war in El Salvador, where he was forced to hide in a latrine from soldiers who raided his town and killed his parents. He later became a faith-based organizer during the civil war, and spent time in prison for his work. He came to the U.S. through the group Doctors Without Borders to have reconstructive surgery on his damaged face.

In his view, conflicts like the civil war in El Salvador as well as global economic policies are the reason many of the laborers are here.

"El Salvador is still suffering because of the war," he said. "A lot of people have left the country. And globalization is behind this whole situation. People are getting poorer and poorer."

*December 4, 2003*

Jesus, a 23-year-old who came to Chicago alone from Acapulco, Mexico in 1999, stands outside a small diner stomping his feet against the cold and burying his hands in the pockets of his red and black jacket. He briefly takes his hands out to pantomime hammering nails into a wall, describing how he worked to help build the casita (little house) that used to be the workers center at the bus turn-around. A 28-year-old man from Michoacan, Mexico with warm eyes and a plaid shirt nods his head in agreement—he too helped build the casita. Not long after it was destroyed by the city to make way for the supposed bike path, the workers were also removed from that site. Despite their determination to stay there, police would come every day and force them to move. So now they are congregating on two corners about a quarter mile away. They have no shelter here, and there is no convenient place for contractors to pick them up. Some contractors double park along the sidewalk, others swing into the small parking lot that the diner shares with a few other businesses. But they must be quick or the officer in the police squad car that sits in the parking lot all day long watching the workers will give them a ticket.

"Lots of contractors are afraid to come here because of the police," said Oscar, the Ecuadorian immigrant, who has remained a key figure in the struggle for a workers center in Albany Park.

Jesus notes that more than three months after the casita was demolished, there has still been no construction on the proposed bike path. He doesn't believe the community or city officials ever really cared that much about a bike path—he sees the plan as a simple excuse to get rid of the workers.

"It's discrimination," he said. "That was just an excuse because they didn't want us around."

This is hardly the first time he has felt discrimination. He's angry that he works so hard and gets only low pay, no health insurance and animosity from U.S. citizens to boot.

"People say immigrants come here to take people's jobs, but that's a lie," he says. "We only do the jobs the gueros (white Americans) don't want to do. Do you think we come here because we want to? We come because we have to, to make a living."

"That would be O.K. if we were paid well, but we're not," added Sergio, a 22-year-old from Cuernavaca, Mexico who came here four years ago, leaving behind a wife and a son who is now seven.

"Some people only want to pay us $5 an hour—not even minimum wage," says Jesus. "They take advantage of Latinos. They might have Americans working at a factory—black, white, whatever, making $15 an hour, and they'll say goodbye, there are no more jobs here, go home. Then they'll hire Latinos for $10 an hour, and they're saving $5 for each person each hour."

Even the jobs that pay better—as much as $15 or $20 an

hour—still never offer any job security or health benefits. Jesus got two nails embedded in his foot at a previous job.

"I got no help to pay the doctor," he said.

Not long after Sergio arrived here, he was working in a restaurant downtown and sliced his right thumb almost off. He cut two nerves, and his whole arm lost feeling. His employers didn't want to pay his hospital bills, though they did end up giving him $1,000 to help cover the accident.

The workers gathered around Sergio listening to his story note that they often have trouble with employers who refuse to pay them for their work. One of the older men waiting on the corner, a short wiry figure in a green and pink Hornets jacket, says that he had worked for the past week and hadn't been paid.

"If they don't pay what can you do?" asked Sergio. "We don't know where they live or who they are. We can make a complaint to the police but they won't do anything since we don't have legal documents."

The workers gathering on this corner around the diner don't feel any more welcomed by certain factions of the neighborhood than when they were at the bus turn-around. They say the local store owners often call the police on them, and if they are drinking coffee in the diner sometimes the police will come and pull them out. Jesus complains that the neighborhood residents who are opposed to the workers center never have meetings with them or come talk to them.

"They are so full of fire, but they never show their faces," he said.

Workers acknowledge that some of the complaints the neighborhood groups have are true—some men do hang out at the workers center to sell drugs, and they often do drink beer there in the evenings in the summer. The charges that they hassle passing women also appear to be true. But they say this isn't reason to dismiss them completely and deny their right to try to make a living.

"Some do sell drugs, but that's not our fault," said Jesus.

"We're hard workers. We just want to survive."

With support from local activist groups, the workers are still trying to get a permanent workers center. But it is a hard fight. They have considered renting a vacant storefront, which used to be a Korean travel agency, next to the diner. But the rent is expensive and workers are having trouble agreeing on the plan. Oscar noted that they are having meetings to discuss five potential locations, but all of them are relatively far from this area.

"Then the contractors won't know where to go to pick us up," noted Jesus. "They're used to coming here. And lots of us live around here, so we can walk to this place. If we have to take a bus, then we'll spend $4 a day on the bus and we might not even get work. We can't afford to do that."

While the workers mill about a white van pulls into the parking lot and a Latino man in a purple sweatshirt jumps out and says, in English, "Who's good with plastic?" Several men clamor into the van and it is gone less than a minute later. After about another hour, a purple car pulls in, hardly stopping as the driver points out several specific men. Sergio is one of them, and he hops quickly into the front seat as the car peels out. At this point the Michoacan native, wearing an Oakland A's baseball cap, has gotten discouraged.

"I've been here 10 years and I don't have a peso in my pocket," he said. "I don't think I'll get any work today."

He and another man decide to head home, as Oscar emerges from the diner where he and a few other workers had been warming themselves.

During the summer waiting for work isn't so bad, because it is warm out and they can relax and socialize. But in the winter it becomes painful. Many of the workers arrive at the site at 6 a.m., and they might wait until 5 p.m. without getting work. Jesus is longing for the warm weather and his family back in Acapulco.

"I really miss it, especially at this time of year, around

Christmas," he says. "I want to go back, but it's too expensive-I'd have to pay a coyote—and then there's the risk of dying walking across the mountains in the cold. Here Christmas is just another day. There's no celebration. I'll just be working."

### Dec. 17, 2003

Today, it is seriously cold out, perhaps the coldest day of the Chicago winter so far. As a result the workers come out later than usual. At 8 a.m. two men from Mongolia are the only ones on the corner, huddling by the edge of the diner. Eric and Arauc were friends in Mongolia and came here together four months ago in search of work. They speak very little English; one of the few phrases that Arauc knows, is "How many guys?" does the contractor need.

They decide to take a break from the cold as more men start arriving. A 22-year-old man named German from Oaxaca, Mexico, whose dress evokes the cholo style of Southern California Chicanos, talks about how rough it was when he arrived in Chicago four years ago.

"The gangbangers shot me four times and broke my bones," he says in English, lifting his sleeves to show ugly puckered scars from the bullets. "It was not so good."

There is almost no work today, since it is so cold. The men stamp their feet and cradle cups of coffee from the diner. A brief diversion is created when one worker accidentally rams his beat-up car into another worker's car across the street. Everyone runs across the street to observe and comment on the situation, and the two men appear to work things out amicably before taking their positions in the line-up waiting for work.

Then Jessica Aranda, a young organizer working with the Latino Union, arrives and greets the men.

She talks about the problem of workers not being paid by contractors.

"It happens because the contractors know the workers aren't organized," she says. "It's also really hard to get them workers compensation, because they have to be able to prove they were working for a specific contractor. One guy fell off a roof and became blind in one eye. We hooked him up with a lawyer, they're trying to do something for him."

She tells the men that a lawyer from the Legal Assistance Foundation will be coming to talk to them about their rights. A little while later the lawyer, an attractive woman in a Muslim head scarf, arrives and the men cluster around eagerly to hear her speech. She gives some basic information and hands out pamphlets and pens. She asks if the men have any questions, but few do. She says that unfortunately because of changes in the foundation's mandate since Sept. 11, they can no longer take the cases of undocumented immigrants—just one more way the world has gotten even harder for these men in the last two years.

While she is talking, German pulls me to the side. His breezy bravado from earlier in the morning is now replaced by complete earnestness and frustration.

"What she's saying is good, but when we go to work and they don't pay us what can we really do?" he asks, in Spanish this time. "These laws she's talking about don't have any effect on us, because the bosses have their own laws. If they don't pay me I can't go to the police, where can I go? A lot of times they don't pay me. If you don't have papers, you don't speak English, they're going to screw you."

For more information:
The National Interfaith Committee for Worker Justice, www.nicwj.org

Lucas Benitez helped the Coalition of Immokalee workers break up several human slavery operations. Photo by Kari Lydersen.

# CHAPTER FOURTEEN

# Pulling Injustice Up From the Roots

## The Coalition of Immokalee Workers

It is 4:30 a.m. in Immokalee, Fla., and suddenly the streets are coming alive.

Under a nearly full moon and a sky full of twinkling stars, figures are stepping out of the palm trees and tall weeds from all directions and heading toward a parking lot illuminated by lights from the La Mexicana #5 grocery store. They walk in twos and threes carrying plastic bags with their lunches. Some of them ride bikes. Soon, as the first faint light begins to show in the sky, old school buses painted red, blue and green begin to pull into the lot. By 5:30 a.m., the place is bustling. There are long lines for coffee and bread inside La Mexicana #5, and ranchera music blares out of an occasional car. Over a hundred men and a small number of women gather in groups and walk from bus to bus, speaking Spanish and Creole. They come from Guatemala, Haiti, Mexico, Honduras, El Salvador and other countries in Latin America; a few of them are African-Americans born in the U.S.

By 6:30 a.m. on this morning in November 2003, the lot is again quiet, save for a few Mayan Indian boys from Guatemala who bicycle by or a pair of Haitian women in bright skirts and head wraps who amble down the street. By this time, most of the workers are on their way to the fields, where they will spend the day picking tomatoes, cucumbers, oranges, watermelons and other fruits and vegetables. The workers earn $40 to

$50 on a good day. The U.S. Department of Labor reported that migrant farm workers earn an average of $7,500 per year, well below the poverty line. Immokalee workers earn even less on average—in 1998 they were found to earn only $6,574 per year.[151]

Up until the 1960's farm workers weren't even covered by minimum wage laws. After that the exemption for farm workers in the Fair Labor Standards Act was overturned, giving them the legal right to minimum wage. But in practice, the minimum wage law is regularly violated through a combination of fraudulent record keeping and virtually non-existent enforcement of labor laws, according to workers advocates.

Farm workers also have no health insurance and virtually no access to workers compensation, and labor law specifically excludes them from the right to organize without fear of retaliation. They also work in close contact with dangerous pesticides on a daily basis, often developing chronic respiratory or skin problems as a result. The growers who own the farms pay contractors to hire farm workers, creating a structure with little accountability and ripe for labor abuses.

It has long been regular procedure for these contractors to fire guns in the air to intimidate workers; to beat them for working too slow or stopping for water; to refuse to pay them their wages. Thousands of workers have recently been toiling in conditions of slavery, forced to work and live under armed guard 24 hours a day.

These workers were literally sold to contractors by the smugglers who helped them cross the border or the ocean into the U.S. They were housed in crowded, shabby trailers or barracks and forced to work fast and hard from sun-up until sundown. They might be paid $40 a week, or less, and from that amount the contractor would subtract money for room and board, leaving them in a constant cycle of debt slavery. If they tried to escape, they were often hunted down and beaten.

Enter the Coalition of Immokalee Workers.

The coalition was formed in 1995 by a group of about 40 workers to combat the gross human rights and labor violations being visited upon the migrant farm workers who come to the town every fall and spring harvest season.

"Immokalee" is a Seminole word for "my home," as a cheerful sign welcoming visitors along the highway points out. It is an hour's drive south of Fort Myers and has a permanent population of about 14,000 that swells to around 30,000 during the harvest seasons.

One of the coalition's first large actions was to rally hundreds of workers to march on the home of a contractor who had beaten a worker severely for trying to get a drink of water. As they marched they held the man's bloody shirt above their heads.

They chanted their slogan, which echoes the mantra of the IWW union's immigrant worker struggles nearly a century ago—"When you strike one of us, you strike us all" ("Golpear a uno es golpear a todos!").

Since that day, there has not been a single report of a contractor beating a worker in the Immokalee area.

The coalition has become an integral part of the community, orchestrating countless marches and protests to demand fair treatment and pay. They intervene in specific cases where a worker is unpaid or abused, and they maintain a constant public presence pressing for better wages and workers' rights. In 2000, they marched 230 miles from Fort Myers to Orlando to protest in front of the Florida Fruit and Vegetable Growers Association. And within the last six years, they have played a critical role in exposing and shutting down five human slavery rings involving a total of over 1,000 workers.[152]

For these achievements, on Nov. 20, 2003 three members of the coalition received the prestigious Robert F. Kennedy Human Rights Award, the first time in its 19-year existence that the prize was given to members of a U.S. organization.

Romeo Ramirez, one of the award recipients, came to

Immokalee six years ago at age 17. He had left his home in Guatemala at age 12 and spent five years on his own working as a farmer and laborer in Chiapas, Mexico.

"I was in Guatemala trying to figure out how to manage," he said. "I could see who were the 'haves' and the 'have-nots.' Even though I was very young this was all clear in my mind."

Almost immediately after he arrived in Immokalee, he heard about the Coalition. He went to one of the meetings, and he was hooked. Here were other people who had the same analysis of the world as him, and they were trying to do something about it.

He told this story on a cool Thursday night in November 2003, as he crouched on the asphalt in the alley behind the coalition's office watching a video being projected on the building's corrugated metal outside wall. It showed him as a skinny teenager newly arrived in the U.S. but already enthusiastically involved in the planning of a protest.

"I was so young then!" he said.

Ramirez played a key role in the November 2002 conviction of three men (themselves immigrants) in Lake Placid, Fla. on federal charges of slavery and extortion which got them a total of 34 years behind bars and the forfeiture of $3 million in assets.[153] Ramirez went undercover in the slavery operation they had been running and spent several weeks working there.

"It was hard work, but it had to be done, whether we were afraid or not," he said of the sting. "I saw the workers being held under armed guard, I saw them prevented from leaving and threatened, it was injustice."

The coalition was also involved in four other slavery investigations and prosecutions going back to 1997. Lucas Benitez, a 28-year-old immigrant from Guerrero, Mexico and another recipient of the award, said there are still numerous cases of slavery in the U.S.

But Benitez and other coalition members note that besides these literal cases of slavery, all farm workers are toiling in such harsh conditions that they often feel like they are slaves.

"Even if there are no armed guards, people are still enslaved by low wages and unhealthy working conditions," said Benitez. "The root of these problems is the same as the root of slavery, the desperation of immigrants to make a living and the way that allows people to exploit them."

To counter this exploitation, the coalition is addressing the problem on a truly grassroots level, involving the farm workers directly with a popular education approach and focusing not only on the conditions of farm workers in the U.S. but on the global economic system that forces so many of them to leave their home countries in the first place. "People say if this is so bad, why don't you find other jobs," said Gerardo Reyes, 26. "But not everyone can run away from the situation. There will always be others who will work, because people are forced into desperate situations. The only way you will change this situation is systematic change. In Mexico people used to grow their crops for subsistence and then sell some of them to make money. Now with all the cheap corn and other grains imported from the U.S. they can't sell any more. So what do they do? That's why I can't follow in the tradition of my father and grandparents."

Reyes's grandparents and his father in Zacatecas, Mexico made their living off the land, growing grains and vegetables in a small farming community. But Reyes realized that would not be an option for him.

"I asked myself the question where do I want to go in life," he said, in fluent English he has learned in just five years in the U.S. "I realized there was not an answer in Zacatecas. If I kept working in the fields in this small town I'd never get out of this cycle of poverty, I might work my whole life and never really be able to provide anything for my family. I wanted to create something, to have something to offer."

So he made it to the U.S., and began working at Immokalee. He found out about the coalition from a co-worker who became his friend and roommate. Soon he was attending coalition meetings and starting to think about things.

"I started to analyze why things are the way they are," he said. "It was an amazing experience for me, to see that there were people here who were fighting against the same things I was against. I learned how an organization works, how people work together to obtain their rights."

Today Reyes along with Benitez, Ramirez and several other workers are staff members of the coalition. And employers no longer feel they can get away with robbing, beating and terrorizing workers. Coalition members say violence and blatant human rights violations have virtually stopped in the area due to their efforts, and if an employer is mistreating or refusing to pay a worker, a visit from the coalition will usually turn the situation around.

"Now things like that don't really happen, because they know if our rights are violated we will march," said Francisca Cortez, a young woman from Oaxaca, Mexico who came here five years ago to work in the fields and is now a staff member at the coalition.

If workers come to at least two of the coalition's weekly meetings, which center heavily on popular education techniques including skits and drawings, workers get a laminated CIW I.D. card. Cortez noted that employers not only in Florida but up the East Coast have learned to have respect for the card.

"In North Carolina a boss told his workers they couldn't have a lunch break," she said. "They showed their CIW cards and he let them. They called us and said, 'The cards even work up here!'"

During a bustling day in the office in November a Guatemalan woman named Lucrecia came in to report that she and her husband along with six other workers had been chased out of the organic squash fields where they were working by a drunken supervisor who was threatening and harassing them. The supervisor claimed they had left voluntarily, and so the workers had not been paid their wages. After a visit from the coalition, the owners of the farm paid the due wages and promised to look into the conduct of the supervisor.

Even with the dent the coalition has made in outright slavery and labor and human rights abuses, however, members are quick to point out that farm workers still live lives of exploitation and abuse. Their wages are hardly any higher than they were 20 years ago. In most areas they pay inordinately high rent for substandard, overcrowded housing close to the work pick-up sites. In Immokalee, the majority of the migrant workers live in a nine-block area adjacent to the parking lot by the Coalition office. They say they pay $35-$50 a week to share a rundown trailer with nine other men or to squeeze onto a bunk bed or mattress in one of the shabby, low-slung apartment complexes with metal doors and crumbling stucco walls.

"There will be six men in these tiny rooms, so all there is room for is the beds," said Cortez, giving a tour of the jumble of trailers and small apartment complexes where workers live. In front of many of the apartment buildings are crude hand-painted signs labeling them as "Campo Gomez" or "Camp Barnhart." At one peach-colored complex right across from the pickup site, "Tenant Only" is stenciled on the doors, and metal grates cover the dingy windows.

"They might look okay on the outside, but inside they are falling apart," says Cortez, who wears three sparkly earrings in each ear and a T-shirt from the Birmingham Civil Rights Institute. "There are rats and cockroaches and no air conditioning. And there is only one stove and one bathroom, so you have to get up at 3 a.m. to wait in line to cook and bathe."

Given the figures provided by Cortez and other workers, the owners of the trailers and apartments would be getting around $1,500 to $2,000 per month for their units, obviously far more than normal market value in the area. Cortez explained that the few local stores in the area are also known to engage in price gouging to take advantage of the workers. So the

Coalition started a co-operative store of its own, where workers can buy tortillas, phone cards, soap, spices and other necessities at just over cost. The co-op is bustling every evening, with workers filing in to pick up some Jumex juice, chiles, cooking oil or whatever else they might want. As they wait in line they gaze at the myriad colorful workers' rights and anti-globalization posters that line the walls. Above the door is a painted slab of wood that reads, "No soy tractor" (I am not a tractor). On an opposite wall is a large mural showing workers from different countries and the words Coalition of Immokalee Workers in English, Spanish and Creole ("Kowalisyon Travaye nan Immokalee"). Next to the racks of black pepper, pumpkin seeds and other goodies sold at the co-op are drawings created in the coalition's popular education workshops, including one of a haughty chihuahua holding a Mexican man on a leash and the words "What's wrong with this picture," a reference to their campaign against Taco Bell.

In fact the huge restaurant chain is the subject of many of the posters and protest signs that make up the pleasant clutter in the office. There are crossed-out chihuahuas with the slogan "Yo no quiero Taco Bell" ("I don't want Taco Bell") and beautifully painted baskets of tomatoes with the slogan "Stop Sweatshops in the Fields." The coalition is demanding that Taco Bell, the largest buyer of tomatoes from Immokalee, pay growers one cent more per pound of tomatoes, which would enable growers to approximately double the pickers' wages. Now, on average a worker must pick two full tons of tomatoes per day to earn $50. They are also asking Taco Bell to facilitate negotiations between growers, contractors and the coalition and to implement a code of conduct mandating fair treatment and wages for pickers.

Targeting major corporations like this is the major focus of the coalition's general strategy for the past few years. Coalition members note that fast food corporations like Taco Bell play a major role in keeping farm workers' wages low, since they pay so little for their produce that growers must look for ways to keep their own costs low.

Benitez addressed the fast food industry's responsibility for the plight of farm workers in his acceptance speech at the Robert F. Kennedy Human Rights Awards in Washington D.C.

"Behind the shiny, happy images promoted by the fast-food industry with its never-ending commercials on TV, fueled by over $3 billion in marketing annually, and behind the supermarket advertising that celebrates the abundance of our harvest each Thanksgiving, there is another reality," Benitez told the crowd. "Behind those images, the reality is that there are farm workers who contribute their sweat and blood so that enormous corporations can profit, all the while living in sub-poverty misery, without benefits, without the right to overtime or protection when we organize."

"If you target these growers, no one knows who they are," added Reyes. "But everyone knows who Taco Bell is. We won't stop targeting the contractors and the growers, but we also want to target the corporations that buy the produce and the consumers who buy the products produced by the corporations."

As of November 2003, Taco Bell had still refused to negotiate with the workers, even after Immokalee workers and their allies led a 10-day hunger strike outside the company's Irvine, Calif. headquarters in February 2003 which gained them the official endorsement of the National Council of Churches. In February 2002 they also did a cross-country "Truth Tour" where they spoke at countless colleges and community centers and got up on tables at Taco Bells throughout the nation to tell the people eating there the true story behind their tomatoes.

The Taco Bell campaign was also a major focus of the Root Cause March in November 2003, a 34-mile trek from Ft. Lauderdale to Miami organized by several south Florida grassroots groups to raise awareness of the effects of free trade on poor communities and people of color. About 50 workers from Immokalee went on the three-day march, which culminated in

Miami for the protests against the FTAA going on at the time.

Thanks to the coalition's efforts there is probably already more awareness about the FTAA per capita in Immokalee than in most major cities. The walls of money transfer outfits, taquerias and apartment buildings are plastered with fliers about the march and the FTAA, and for a week before the march the coalition handed out free coffee and bread along with fliers about the FTAA to workers starting at 4 in the morning.

"Senores, the time has arrived for the free coffee," Ramirez called out over a megaphone into the chilly darkness the morning before the march, quickly drawing crowds of workers over from the parking lot where the buses were waiting to take them to the fields. As they got coffee, bread and steaming cups of oatmeal, Ramirez said, "This is the last day to sign up for the march to Miami. If you can't come on the march, please learn this information about the FTAA. It will make the rich richer and the poor poorer."

The next evening at the pre-march meeting, it was obvious his early morning message and the rest of the campaign had had an effect. The room was filled with men and a handful of women ready to go on the march; some of them long-time coalition members and some in the office for the first time.

Some reclined wearily on the couches, others leaned forward with excitement on the folding chairs.

"I'm not afraid, this will be a good march," said a middle-aged man from Veracruz, Mexico still covered in mud from his day in the fields.

"We get paid so little, it's a crime," said Amilcar Cruz, 26, a Guatemalan who had come to the office for the first time. "That's why I'm marching, for our rights. We are humans too!"

Awareness of human slavery and governmental attention to the problem is definitely on the rise, thanks largely to the Immokalee workers and other activists. The U.S. Justice Department says that the number of human trafficking cases being prosecuted has increased three-fold in the last three years, with 125 such cases currently under investigation.[154]

In December 2003, *The Palm Beach Post* made public an ongoing Department of Justice investigation into the enslavement of immigrant tomato-pickers in the town of Wimauma, Florida, several hours drive from Immokalee. A 28-year-old Mexican immigrant who received temporary legal status for cooperating with the FBI described the situation: "The contractors, afraid the workers would try to escape, began to guard them at all times and, on some occasions when no guard was available, locked them in a trailer that was secured with a thick chain, a padlock and windows that were nailed so that no one could get out."[155]

While Justice Department investigations focus specifically on the contractors involved in running slavery operations, the coalition members see raising awareness about the FTAA and the role of corporations like Taco Bell in the oppression of workers as just as much a part of the struggle for human rights as their work exposing slavery.

"When they've been negotiating something in secret for over six years, with the investors and the people who own companies, when they're trying to change the constitutional laws of countries to favor the people with money and power, you know there's nothing good about it," said Reyes. "They're not asking the poor, they're not asking the needy and the hungry, instead they're making their money off the poor. A lot of people in Mexico, in poor countries around the world, don't know [about the FTAA]. But we know we are poor, and we just need to ask ourselves why. The answer is the FTAA, free trade and corruption. That's why we're taking to the streets and making our voices heard."

One of the Immokalee workers marching to Miami was Mathieu Beaucicot, who came to the U.S. from Haiti in 1992 looking for a better life. He left a wife and five daughters behind.

"I work so hard for almost no money," said Beaucicot, 48,

in Spanish he has learned from his fellow workers, with a soft Caribbean lilt from his native Creole. "After I pay for rent and food I have no money left to send back to my family. In Haiti there was no money and the work was hard but you could have a beer, relax, spend time with your family. Here all you do is work. I work when I'm tired, I work when I'm sick and I get no Medicaid, no Social Security, no health insurance."

As is the case with most of the workers who come through the coalition offices, it is clear that the hours of hard work haven't dimmed Beaucicot's spirit. He is quick to smile and laugh—and play a mean game of dominoes, his friends note—carrying on the fight with a spirit of gentleness and joy.

"We will just keep fighting more and more," he said. "We're used to working hard."

For more information:

The Coalition of Immokalee Workers, www.ciw-online.org.

National Center for Farmworker Health, www.ncfh.org.

Miguel Ibarra has gone from being one of only a few Latinos in Schuyler, Nebraska, to one of thousands. Photo by Kari Lydersen

# CHAPTER FIFTEEN

# Longing for Home; Hoping to Stay

## An Immigrant's Life in Nebraska

### In Omaha, Longing For Home:

Relaxing on the wooden porch of their house in Omaha, Nebraska, across the street from a park where a group of Mexicans are playing soccer and just down the block from a Mexican cantina called Bar California, Chano, Nemo, Noe and Juan are a long way from home.

All four are from the small town of Mixquiahuala de Juarez in the state of Hidalgo, about a 30-hour bus ride or 18-hour car ride from the U.S.-Mexico border. They all desperately want to return to their hometown, where they have left behind children, parents, wives, brothers and sisters. But there is no work to be had in their farming community of about 2,500 people. There are others from their town here in Omaha too.

"If you have a business [in Hidalgo] you can survive, but if you don't have a job you have nothing," says Chano, 22, on an afternoon in August 2003. He wears a yellow baseball cap jauntily backwards over his round face. He came here with his wife three years ago.

The displaced residents of Mixquiahuala are just a few of a huge migration of Mexican and other Latin American immigrants who have ended up in small towns and cities in Nebraska and throughout the midwest in the past few years.

In Nebraska, the Latino population increased 155 percent between the 1990 and 2000 census, for a total of 94,425 in 2000. And this number is likely a significant undercount, since undocumented immigrants and immigrants in general are traditionally undercounted by the census. In fact, Nebraska is seventh in the nation in terms of the growth in Latino population during the '90s, after North Carolina, Georgia, Nevada, Arizona, Utah and Tennessee. This largely explains why between 1990 and 2000 Nebraska saw its largest population gain in 80 years, growing 8.5 percent to 1.7 million people.[156]

This changed the state's population from almost completely white to having a significant Latino population. In Omaha, the state's largest metropolitan center, the change is evident from the Mexican grocery stores, bars and other businesses that now line the streets. In 1990 Omaha was home to 10,228 Latinos, out of a total population of 335,719. By 2000 the Latino population had almost tripled to 29,397 out of the 390,007 total population.[157] And more immigrants are arriving from Mexico, Central America or other parts of the U.S. every day.

Many Mexican and Central America immigrants have come to work in the city's three slaughterhouses—Nebraska Beef, Swift, and IBP. There used to be 12 meatpacking plants in the city, staffed by a workforce of European immigrants, but today automation and assembly line techniques mean the same volume of work is done by only three plants and workers are paid much less for this "unskilled" work than the Europeans earned for their "skilled" work. The government has estimated that a quarter of the state's meatpacking workforce is undocumented, but local agencies say the total is at least double that number.[158]

The Mixquiahuala natives here send money back to Mexico for friends and family to pay the $1,500 to $1,800 fees for coyotes to help them cross the border, and then once they arrive in Omaha they help them fill out job applications and find a place to live. Now the four men live along with Nemo's brother and Chano's wife and cousin in the somewhat run-down but comfortable wooden house in a neighborhood that is home to many Mexicans as well as Sudanese refugees and

African-Americans. Before they moved to this house, they were all living in two rooms in a basement where it was hard to stand up straight. Like most immigrants in Omaha and in small towns across the country, they work up to 17 hours a day, often in two jobs, to send money back to their families in Mexico.

Juan, 34, and Noe, 29, are currently only working one job each, at a plant that turns lumber into trimmed logs and pays a good wage of about $12.50 an hour. Their nine hours or so of work a day leave them some time and energy to play soccer or do grocery shopping. But in the past, both worked two jobs every day, at the lumber plant in the morning and cleaning offices at night, for a total of about 17 hours of work daily. They would work at the lumber company from about 7 am to 3 pm, then they would clean offices from 5 pm to about 1:30 am.

"I only slept three or four hours a night for three years," notes Noe. "I was very tired, physically and mentally."

Nemo, 34, currently works two jobs, at Burger King and doing construction. Juan's 16-year-old nephew also works at Burger King. Meanwhile Chano works laying cement "steps, stoops and sidewalks," some of the words he can say in English. He earns about $9 an hour.

"A lot of Mexicans work in concrete," he says.

Juan didn't want to come to Omaha, but he wanted to build a better house for his parents, who were living in a two-room earthen structure where the walls were falling down. He talked to his friend Noe, who has been in Omaha for six years.

"Noe said to come here, that there is opportunity here," he says. "He convinced me to come. Now my parents live in a home with cinder block walls."

Their hometown is "puro campo," or pure country, the men note. There is no industry and the main revenue comes from people growing corn, beans and calabazas. Now, the town is home largely to women, since "the majority" of the men, in Noe's words, have migrated.

"[Their town] is a lot different now," said Noe. "It's almost all women. The men don't want to go to the U.S., but it's nec-essary for them to be able to buy the products their families need, their babies need."

Nemo has a three-year-old daughter, but he's only seen her for four months in between his four different stays in Omaha. He originally came to Omaha about six years ago and stayed for a year, then with visits to Mexico in between he has lived in Omaha for three stretches of one or two years each. Nemo's brother Jose Luis, who has been in the U.S. for eight years on and off, is in a similar situation. During the Super Bowl this year, at half time the men popped in a video Jose Luis's wife had sent from Mexico showing the daughter he barely knows.

"He went home, got married and had a child," says Nemo of his brother. "Then he had to come back here to earn money to support his daughter. It's very sad being here. I can't enjoy my daughter, my family. I talk to my family two times a week. I miss them a lot."

Noe crossed the border in California in the trunk of a car. Immigration officials stopped the car, and the other riders were detained. They didn't know he was in the trunk.

"The agents were calling out and I didn't answer," he says. "Later they came back and I still didn't answer."

After hiding in the sealed trunk for hours, Noe kicked his way out through the back seat and got out, finding himself alone in the desert. He walked about six kilometers until he found help.

"There was nothing around, nobody," he says. "I was afraid. It's very dangerous."

Chano came in a freight train's boxcar, another common and dangerous route. In September 2002, the decomposing bod-ies of 11 immigrants who had been trying to make a similar trek were found in a sealed boxcar in Denison, Iowa, not too far away from Omaha.[159]

"I was three days without water or food," says Chano.

One time when Nemo was crossing through the desert, his

small group saw Border Patrol agents nearby so they hid in a ditch and covered themselves with brambles.

"But the brambles had thorns on them so we were all cut up," he says.

Nemo hopes to visit his family in about six months.

"It's a question whether I'll be able to get back across or not," he says. "Maybe yes, maybe no—we'll see."

Many Mexicans they knew in Omaha have not been able to get back into the U.S. after going to Mexico for visits. This has had an effect on the workforce at the lumber plant, where about half the 50-person workforce used to be Mexican. Now there are only nine Mexicans working there, Noe said.

Deportation is a constant possibility, though the men say they don't worry about it too much, they have an attitude that given all they've been through so far, whatever will be will be. They don't really consider long-term residence in the U.S. a possibility, since as of now they can't even get drivers licenses, no less green cards.

"Without an identity it is hard to make a life," says Noe. "How can your heart be somewhere where you don't count, where you legally don't even exist?"

## In Schuyler: Here to Stay

"Looking good, old man!" Miguel Ibarra, 41, calls out to an older white man driving by in a pickup.

"He just had open heart surgery," Ibarra explains, perched on a bench outside the Latino Club and Latino Restaurant on the cobble-stoned main drag of the small town of Schuyler, Nebraska. Almost everyone who drives by, white or Latino, greets Ibarra warmly or waves out a truck window.

As of August 2003, Ibarra has been in Schuyler for 16 years, all of it spent working at the Excel meatpacking plant. He has seen a lot of changes in that time. When he first arrived here from New Mexico, where he had immigrated from Mexico

25 years ago, he said there were only a few Latinos in the whole area.

Today, the town is 50 percent Latino or more, mostly Mexicans and some Guatemalans and Puerto Ricans.

The 1990 census counted 164 Latinos out of the 4,052 population, whereas by 2000 the census counted 2,423 Latinos out of 5,371.

The majority of businesses are Mexican or Guatemalan—the main drag is home to the Latino Club and Latino Restaurant; the Taco and Burrito King taco shop; San Miguel Liquors and Mexican and Guatemalan groceries with colorful pinatas dangling from the ceilings.

Many of the Mexican immigrants have come to work at Excel, which currently has about 80 percent Latino employees, according to Ibarra.

Ibarra originally migrated to New Mexico by crossing the border near El Paso, Texas with his father to work in a mica (mineral) milling operation, then on a visit to his in-laws in Nebraska he found out about Excel. When he first started at Excel, where he is now a training supervisor, there were only 10 Mexican employees. Along with Mexicans there are now a lot of Guatemalans and some Hondurans, Puerto Ricans and other Latinos. The pay, $10.20 to $12.35 an hour, allows people to save money to send home. The plant also offers free English classes to residents, and workers are trying to get a day care center established.

"In 1995 it just exploded," Ibarra says of the immigrant population. "Now you see the change in the plant and in the community. You see all the Mexican businesses, we've started buying homes. Ninety percent of new home sales are to Hispanics."

He notes that many Mexican immigrants come from the farming town of Chichihualco in the southern state of Guerrero, one of Mexico's poorest and most rural areas. The immigrants in Schuyler work together to send money back to their hometowns for various projects. For example, their funds have helped build churches and allowed the purchase of an ambulance.

Ibarra, who speaks fluent English, notes that it is important to the immigrants here to keep their culture and ties with Mexico alive, especially for the children who come here as babies and grow up more American than Mexican.

"We teach the kids the dances from Guerrero, we make sure they know about the culture," he says.

He helped found a group called Latinos Unidos to work on political and cultural issues—currently they are carrying out a voter registration drive for Mexicans who have become U.S. citizens and they are trying to pass a bond issue to provide more money to the overcrowded schools. He notes that there is not a single Latino elected official in the town, though they recently had a victory in a Mexican being named to the Board of Directors of the local hospital.

"In Mexico the schools are paid for by the government but here we need to pay for them [through taxes]," he notes. "There are too many kids in the classrooms, they don't retain as much."

Meanwhile the schools are now about 80 to 90 percent Latino students, according to Jim DeBlauw, head administrator for Schuyler's two elementary schools. They gain about 50 students per year, as new immigrants move in or families have more children. One school houses kindergartners and first graders while the other is second through eighth grade. At lunch time during the first week of school in late August, first graders file into the lime green-painted lunch room in perfect order and pick up lunch trays at a window before sitting in perfect rows at the cafeteria tables. They giggle and talk in Spanish and English.

DeBlauw notes that most white parents now send their children to the "country schools" outside Schuyler. He says about 70 parents have "opted out" of Schuyler's schools, most of them white.

This is one of the signs of fear or a lack of understanding on the part of long-time white residents. Ed Leahy, the sole paid organizer of the Iowa-Nebraska Immigrants Rights Network, notes that there are others—for example he said the Schuyler Chamber of Commerce's book of business listing doesn't include a single Mexican business and the letters section of the local paper often contains white residents' rants about Mexicans drinking beer or letting their children run around naked. When four men of Mexican descent, who were actually U.S. citizens, killed five people during a bank robbery in nearby Norfolk on Sept. 26, 2002, racial tensions in the area were stirred.[160]

"Many issues still need to be addressed to better reflect unity in the community, like representing the many Hispanic businesses in the local Chamber of Commerce's directory and limiting the impact of white flight from the schools," says Leahy. "But Schuyler is looked at as a proving ground for inclusiveness in the area."

Ann Naffier, an immigration specialist at the American Friends Service Committee in Des Moines who works closely with Leahy, said most people in small towns have a genuine desire to welcome new immigrants, but at the same time struggle with their own preconceptions.

"A nice white lady might be perfectly fine with immigrants, until someone plays a kind of music she doesn't like or parks cars on the lawn," she said.

She noted that a local woman scolded two immigrant siblings for being affectionate with each other outside the church, thinking they were boyfriend and girlfriend.

"She was from good German stock where you don't come within two feet of another person," said Naffier. "She was incredibly embarrassed when I told her they were brother and sister, and that people are a lot closer to their siblings in Mexico."

Overall, according to Leahy and many immigrant residents, the ethnic change in the neighborhood has gone well and residents have made real efforts to resolve conflicts and increase understanding.

"When racial tensions in the area rose after the bank robbery last fall, the vast majority of the community responded positively to calls for peace," says Leahy.

The shift has been helped along by the vital economic role the Mexican residents play in the community and the small town hospitality of long time residents.

"There have been some incidents, but those are isolated and there's almost always alcohol involved," Ibarra says of racial problems. "The Anglos saw us coming, and later they realized we weren't leaving, so they decided to adopt us."

Cristobal Salinas and his wife Josefina and two teenage sons are among the residents who are glad to have made a home in Schuyler. They run the Taco and Burrito King restaurant on the town's main drag, which bustles with customers every lunch hour. The wall behind the counter is lined with phone cards which customers can buy to call Mexico. They came here from their hometown of Atolinga in the state of Zacatecas after Cristobal was the victim of an armed robbery in which his hands and feet were bound with masking tape and he was held at gunpoint.

"After that I was afraid for the safety of my children, and a year later we came here," says Cristobal, who was in the construction business in Mexico.

Several of his brothers were already in the U.S.—the family runs five Taco and Burrito king restaurants in Chicago along with one in Madison, Nebraska. He studied cooking for two years and then opened his restaurant two years ago. The whole family works there, and they say it has been a huge success. They are part of the Club Social Atolinga, a group of Atolinga natives with members all over the U.S. who send money back to their hometown for projects. Cristobal shows off a glossy magazine with ads for the Taco and Burrito King and other members' businesses along with articles and photos of the projects they have built in Atolinga. There is an elegant stone social club, a sports center and other beautiful buildings. He notes that there are now more Atolinga residents in the U.S.—he estimates 5,000 to 6,000—then there are in Atolinga, which has a population of 1,756. Though Cristobal and his family maintain strong ties to Atolinga, they consider the U.S. their home. Especially considering his experience with the armed robbery, Cristobal is a big fan of the U.S.'s justice system and culture.

"In [Atolinga] there were a lot of people with bad intentions," he says. "Here the laws are very just, everyone who's visited us has been very nice. This has been a success."

For more information:

Iowa-Nebraska Immigrant Rights Network, through the AFSC: www.afsc.org/central/ia.

Nebraska Appleseed: www.neappleseed.org.

# PROFILES

Jose Oliva's family fled persecution in Guatemala. Photo by Kari Lydersen.

# CHAPTER SIXTEEN

# Jose Oliva
## Coming Full Circle

Growing up in Xela, Guatemala, Jose Oliva always knew he would be a fighter for social justice.

His grandfather was a key official in the government of President Jacob Arbenz, helping to draft the political and economic policies necessary to transition the country from a capitalist to socialist economy in the early 1950s.

His father and aunt were internationalist guerrilla fighters who joined the revolutions in Nicaragua and Guatemala—his aunt was killed in Nicaragua by the U.S.-backed Contras. And his mother was a community organizer and school teacher.

"I hear high school students talk about what they want to do with their lives and it feels kind of strange because it was never a question to me," he said. "I always knew if I didn't devote my entire life to this struggle I'd be betraying my people. I never had a doubt in my mind."

His grandfather, Mario Francisco Gonzalez Orellana, was exiled to the mountain town of Xela from Guatemala City after the Arbenz regime was toppled in a C.I.A.-orchestrated coup in 1954. His mother was born that year, and 18 years later Oliva was born.

In 1985, they were forced to flee the country altogether after his mother got death threats from the paramilitary group Jaguar Justicio (Jaguar of Justice).

"She was a teacher, and after school she'd stay and talk to the parents about their issues," said Oliva, 31. "Their number one priority was getting running water and electricity, so my mom's goal was to figure out how to help them do that. That was her crime. That's what got her branded a Communist."

He said everyone knew the paramilitary group was indistinguishable from the army. When they left his mother a note saying she had 24 hours to leave or be killed, the family took it seriously. Through family connections they were able to make their way to Miami.

"The only reason I'm here today, the only reason our whole family wasn't massacred, was our class," noted Oliva. "We were middle class, so we were able to leave."

Oliva's grandfather also died shortly before they left the country. Oliva noted that in the ensuing years, he took to heart one of the lessons his grandfather had always taught him—to question everything.

"He would help me study history, and he told me to always remember everything they tell you in school, and then not to believe any of it."

After a short time in Miami and Orlando his family moved to Chicago where they had some friends.

As a 12-year-old newly arrived in the U.S., he found that the social position he had enjoyed growing up in Guatemala as a ladino, or person of mixed Spanish and indigenous heritage, was flipped on its head.

"I had always been on the dishing side of racism, there are these very clear cut castes in Guatemala and as a ladino I was always treated better, always rushed to the front of the line. Then all of a sudden I was on the receiving end of racism, because I was the immigrant. There was this dynamic in the schools where the black kids were just on their own, no one messed with them, and the white kids and the (second-generation) Latinos interacted but in a strange way. The white boys kind of looked up to the Latino boys and thought they were cool, and the Latino girls kind of wanted to be like the white girls. Then there was this under layer of immigrants, and whether you were from India or Guatemala or whatever you were messed with. That really got me thinking about the way Mayans are treated in Guatemala, and about my own Mayan heritage."

He also saw his parents, who had been part of the educated middle class in Guatemala, struggle to eke out an existence as refugees.

"It was really hard for a while," he said. "My mother was working at 7-11 and my father was basically unemployed. A lot of times we had to choose between paying the rent and buying groceries."

Despite his steadfast devotion to a legacy of activism, like many teenagers he began to suffer an identity crisis. He joined a gang in Albany Park, the northwest side Chicago neighborhood where his family lived, and became a talented bike thief with the nickname Chino, a reference to what his friends saw as his vaguely Asian appearance.

"I did all the crazy stuff, it was kind of a statement of rebellion," he said, noting that only a few of the crowd of 20 or so boys he hung out with avoided being killed or incarcerated.

Several years later he left the gang lifestyle. He said there was no simple reason why he left, but part of the shift was his discovery of spirituality, something his Marxist, atheist parents had always scorned. He calls his father a "born again atheist" whose rejection of religion was so strong that he would evangelize atheism just like others tried to spread the gospel.

A Guatemalan friend and mentor named Julio took him to his first sweat lodge and Sundance, Native American traditions which have also been embraced by indigenous people from other countries. He briefly hooked up with a group called Youth Struggling for Survival which uses indigenous spirituality as a vehicle to help "at risk" urban youth.

"But all the time I was in the gang and then getting involved in spirituality, I never left my family's identity as radical combatants," he said.

His parents were primarily connected with the secular pan-American leftist group PRTC (Partido Revolucionario de los Trabajadores Centroamericanos/ Revolutionary Party of

Central American Workers), but that along with other resistance groups merged into the ORPA (Organizacion del Pueblo en Armas/ Armed Organization of the People), which Oliva describes as having "an interesting mix of anarchism, spirituality and Marxism."

"So it was almost like I had planned getting into all this spirituality to come full circle and get closer to what my parents had been involved in," he said.

He became increasingly connected in the Guatemalan community in Chicago, becoming executive director of the organization Casa Guatemala and starting a weekly radio show called The Voice of Guatemala on a college radio station. After meeting activist and writer Jennifer Harbury, whose husband was murdered during the Civil War in Guatemala, he helped obtain donated radio equipment from around the U.S. to send to Guatemala.

"At this point in time it was all perfect, my life was all making sense."

But, of course, it wasn't that easy. Oliva began to feel frustrated by the fact that he seemed to be always preaching to the converted within the Guatemalan and leftist communities, and his world of clear cut black-and-white, right-and-wrong began to fall apart. To top it off, the Casa Guatemala office was burnt to the ground in what many still suspect was a case of arson.

"I gained the sophistication of seeing that things don't always happen for a reason," Oliva said.

He began to shift the nature of his activism, to try to reach out to a larger circle of people, people who didn't necessarily see the world in the same way he did.

"We have a few choices in our work," he said. "We can be puritanical and stick to our ideals to the point of being ineffective. Or we can be realistic and say, 'I can't change everyone in an instant, but I can try to understand them where they are at and meet them there."

This shift led him eventually to his current job, as director of the Workers Center for the Chicago Interfaith Committee on Worker Issues. Here, he works with religious leaders to support workers in their struggles to unionize or fight labor abuses and discrimination. A major focus of his job is to establish and support workers centers, places where day laborers—most of them immigrants—can congregate to be hired for temporary jobs and subvert the highly exploitative temp agencies that pepper the streets in immigrant neighborhoods. He has traveled around the country learning about and advising other workers centers, and others in the workers center movement have described Oliva as a national leader.

In this context, you could say he has truly come full circle. One of his major campaigns has been working with Latin American immigrants to form the workers center in Albany Park, the same neighborhood where he grew up almost two decades ago.

"Things don't all make sense anymore," he said. "I'm not doing my dream job—I'm working with religious institutions and I'm not religious [as in organized religion]; I'm working with labor unions and people that are far more conservative than I am. But I feel like this is so effective. I can see change daily."

Alexy Lanza sees himself as an internationalist fighting for the
rights of immigrants in the U.S. and people all over the world.
Photo by Kari Lydersen.

# CHAPTER SEVENTEEN

# Alexy Lanza
## "Wherever I See Injustice..."

$A$s a 21-year-old in Honduras, Alexy Lanza felt like he had been fighting and dodging oppressive forces for most of his young life. Military service was mandatory and if a young man didn't voluntarily show up for their service, military officials would hunt them down and conscript them.

"When you'd go to the bars in the poor areas they'd come and catch you and make you do your military service," he said. "They'd even enter your home to find you. You weren't free to go see a movie because you'd be afraid they'd take you."

Lanza was tired of living on the run, so he decided to volunteer for the Air Force, where at least he would have the opportunity to learn technical and tactical skills. But he clashed constantly with his commanders.

"I was one of those bad guys who didn't like to follow orders," he said.

After two and a half years in the military, he worked at a factory called Serviciera Hondurena bottling Salvavida, the national beer, Coca-Cola and other beverages. The union workers decided to go on strike, but as a temporary hire Lanza wasn't legally allowed to participate.

"If I participated in the strike I would be fired, so I decided to participate in the strike," he said.

The government intelligence agency put him under surveillance because of his labor activism, and soon he was "having experiences with these guys trying to tell me things with guns."

Lanza's family was slightly better off than most; his mother was a peasant who had migrated from the country and his father was a teacher from a middle class family.

"We had a good life but we were part of the working class," he said.

He was always aware of the economic inequality that existed in the country, where poor people living in the marginalized parts of the cities or the country were treated as second class citizens and regularly suffered abuse at the hands of authorities while struggling to eke out a living. The political situation was especially tense at the time because Honduras was flooded with right-wing Contras fleeing Nicaragua, where the leftist Sandistas had just taken over. Lanza noted that the Contra sympathizers were warmly welcomed by the Honduran government, and seemed to always have the nicest homes and openly carried weapons.

"Imagine seeing a guy with two AKs on a motorcycle riding around the neighborhood," he said. "The Contras had more power than even the police. They could carry any type of gun and do whatever they wanted. When somebody tried to organize a demonstration or something, they'd be disappeared."

So he embarked on what would be an eight-month odyssey which eventually landed him in Chicago, after being imprisoned, deported, robbed and trekking through remote parts of Latin America, surviving only through his wits and the hospitality of indigenous communities in the mountains of Guatemala and Mexico.

He first crossed illegally from Honduras to Guatemala on a bus with his friend and three cousins. In Guatemala they had various run-ins with the military. They spent 18 hours walking through mountains and a huge banana plantation. One of his cousins and his friend gave up, but the other three kept walking. Finally they made it to the border across from the Mexican town of Tapachula and crossed at night. They were in a small bus when Mexican soldiers boarded and pulled them off. They were deported, but crossed back over that same day with three Guatemalans they had met. Then when they were in a small town near San Cristobal in the Mexican state of Chiapas, they were robbed of all their belongings.

"Everyday you see people from Central America crossing there, and people know we have money," he said. "So some groups decided to have fun with this, and we were one of the victims."

They had accepted an offer to stay with a man, who cooked food for them and told them they'd leave at 3 am for their next stop.

"He came for us with a machete, and then we found three more guys, one with a gun and two with machetes. They said, 'Show me the money baby,'" said Lanza with a resigned laugh. "So we gave them all our money and they left us there."

Luckily one of the Guatemalans had hidden a little cash inside the leather of his shoe, so they were able to get on a bus. They lived from day to day finding people who would give them housing or food, until they were picked up by immigration authorities yet again near the border with the state of Oaxaca. They were put in jail by the same officials who had deported them the previous time.

"They said if we see you again we won't let you go," he said. Since they were penniless, they worked for about a month in Guatemala before setting off on the trip again. This time they crossed at a less heavily guarded border in the (Mexican) state of Yucatan and evaded immigration by traveling through remote stretches of mountains and staying with different isolated indigenous communities, some of them who didn't speak a word of Spanish.

"It was such a beautiful experience, meeting all these different people and visiting these indigenous communities," he said. "I always tried to experience the moment fully. I kept a diary of the people we met and the things we did. I remember in Oaxaca working with the people and seeing one guy kill a couple snakes."

Finally they made it to Mexico City, where they spent

another stretch working to earn money. The Guatemalans stayed there, having "met some girls," so Lanza and his two cousins headed on to the border between Ciudad Juarez and El Paso, Texas. They worked for a month in Juarez to earn money.

"It was hard because we were spending all the money we earned just to sleep and eat," he said. "I just got tired and said I'm going to cross the border."

His cousins, who were both older, didn't believe him. But he did it. Compared to all their past travails, "it was a piece of cake."

A few men hiding in a tree near the border signaled to him and told him to join them in sneaking into a train car. It would be the 19th attempted crossing for one of the men. They crossed on July 4, since many of the police and Border Patrol agents had that day off.

They made a hole in the wall of one of the cars and hid, above the passenger compartment. They were without food or water for two and a half days. Then they got off in a town in Kansas for water and hot dogs, and the other men bolted. Lanza didn't like Kansas, so he continued on. He traveled in a boxcar to Chicago with a Mexican man who knew all the train routes, then separated with him in Chicago after the man tried to rob someone.

Today Lanza is still in Chicago, as a legal resident. He is married with a three-year-old daughter named Violeta, and makes a living doing painting and construction. He quickly hooked up with an immigrant community of activists and artists in the city, and early on got involved with political art and music. He is an experienced print-maker, video-maker and photographer, he sang with a collective playing "nuevo troba" protest music and he worked with political street theater projects. He recently completed an album of Pablo Neruda poems put to indigenous music, in conjunction with the band Raiz Viva. He even traveled to Palestine in the summer of 2002 to meet with groups in the occupied territories and take photos and video. One of the photos he has sold to raise money for these groups shows the ragged frame of a destroyed television set framing a scene of bombed out buildings in Jenin.

He sees this all as his form of resistance, a way of thanking all the people who helped him during his journey and a way to contribute to the struggle for peace and prosperity in Honduras and the rest of Latin America.

"I see photography, video, poetry and everything as a way to express the feelings, hopes, pain and suffering of my people," he said.

Lanza has visited his family in Honduras several times since gaining legal residency in the U.S.—they still see him as the lovably crazy son. He sees the poverty and repression in Honduras getting worse and worse.

He noted that Honduras is a rural country, with about three quarters of the population living as farmers. But it is getting harder and harder for these farmers to make a living.

"Now you have all these transnational companies that can produce food much more cheaply, so the farmers growing corn and coffee can't sell their crops. If they sell at the same prices as the transnationals, they'll actually lose money. Most of them have borrowed money from the bank to buy their seeds and tools, so if they can't pay the bank back they lose their land which the bank was holding as collateral."

Once displaced, many are migrating to the cities to work in the maquilas that are popping up, particularly in San Pedro Sula, the country's most modern city.

"Then the farmers who leave the land end up as the poorest and most marginalized in the cities," he said. "It has an economic impact on both sides, the country and the cities. The government gives the transnationals free land but they will never pass a law to help the peasants."

He notes that there is a popular saying that while the current president, Ricardo Maduro, has declared a war on poverty, "the way he will do it is by killing the poor."

He sees hope, however, because he thinks the campesinos and the general population are more organized than ever before.

"That has a lot to do with what's happening around the world, the Zapatistas, what's going on in Argentina and Venezuela. People can see the similarities and explore different ways to organize."

Besides his art, one of Lanza's main projects in Chicago is working with the solidarity group La Voz de los de Abajo—"the voice of those below." The small group works closely with a campesino group in Honduras and other Latin American organizations to publicize what's going on in their communities and help them raise funds.

"Wherever I see injustice, I vow to fight it," he said.

Living and raising a child in the U.S., he has to deal with the contradictions of an immigrant's life.

"When immigrants come to this country, we have two choices," he noted. "We can lose our identity or we can make it stronger. You lose it when you see all the wealth here and you think I want to have a big car, a nice house, this and that. You start forgetting little by little where you came from."

"But you have to remember that all these riches are made from the poverty of our countries, from what was taken from us. When you realize that, then your roots become strong. My roots were strong already. But they truly became strong here."

Neris Gonzalez escaped torture and persecution in El Salvador to found an urban gardening project called Ecovida in Chicago. Photo by Kari Lydersen.

# CHAPTER EIGHTEEN

# Neris Gonzalez
## The Seeds of Change

W hen Neris Gonzalez was about seven years old, the president of El Salvador visited her school in San Nicolas Lempa, a village in the state of San Vicente, El Salvador. "We all waited in line to receive him, holding flowers," she said.

The president made a remark about "campesinos tontos," or foolish peasants, and everyone cheered. Everyone except young Neris, one of 12 children in a campesino family.

"I had walked two hours to school to meet him, and we were holding flowers from our own gardens, and he called us tontos," said Gonzalez, now 49. "Everyone was cheering, but I was so angry."

When she got home she asked her grandmother how the president could call them that name. "Because we are poor," said her grandmother. "And we don't know how to read and write."

"But we have a mountain of things," Gonzalez remembers saying, meaning the fruit trees and animals that flourished in their small community. "I was 100 percent campesina, but I was proud of my origins. I grew up in poverty, but I was rich in health, rich in nurturing."

She became driven to understand why the president would make such a statement about her people, and to prove him wrong. "I spent years trying to understand the word tontos, and every year I understood more and more," she said.

Though it wasn't normal for all children to go to school, especially girls, she walked two hours to school every day and studied voraciously. When she got older she began teaching classes to other students and campesinos.

Meanwhile, the sting of inequality that Gonzalez had sensed in the president's words was also being felt around the country, and people were refusing to take it anymore. A popular resistance to the corrupt and repressive government was growing.

In her early 20s Gonzalez got involved with a church group that was doing health and literacy work with the campesinos. Many people existed in a plantation-like system at the time, working for large landowners and selling their crops to them. The landowners would regularly shortchange the peasants, undercounting the amount of beans or grains they were selling. Gonzalez and others with the church realized that by teaching basic counting and reading skills to the campesinos, they could get fair pay for their work.

"I taught them to read, to count from one to 100," Gonzalez said.

The country was now on the verge of civil war, which would fully break out in 1980 between the U.S.-backed government and the FMLN guerrilla army. By the time peace accords were signed in 1992, over 75,000 people would be killed or disappeared in the war, including countless civilians aligned with nonviolent church groups and community organizations. In the eyes of the government, the literacy work Gonzalez was doing amounted to revolutionary subversion. She and her cohorts got threats from the paramilitary groups who were intimidating, disappearing and torturing dissidents and church workers at the behest of the government. On March 22, 1977, Gonzalez's mentor Father Rutilio Grande was murdered by right-wing forces. On December 26, 1979, Gonzalez, who was pregnant at the time, was kidnapped in broad daylight in the market near San Nicolas Lempa.

She was held by the death squads at a National Guard Post in the city of San Vicente for two weeks, where she was raped, tortured and forced to watch the mutilation of a young boy. She was finally dumped unconscious in a ditch, and a neighbor brought her back to her family. It took her weeks to regain her memory, and her newborn son died two months after birth because of the effects of torture. International connections she had made through the church offered to help her get asylum abroad, but now the fire was really lit in Gonzalez. She picked up her work advocating for and educating the poor, among other things traveling to the capitol San Salvador to demand more funding for community programs. The tiny country was now devastated environmentally and economically by the civil war.

"Whole towns had been destroyed by napalm which they would drop from planes," she said, showing a small scar from napalm on her ankle. "It was like the second Vietnam. After the napalm was dropped the earth was scalded, nothing could grow anymore. The rivers were drained, the land was arid, the forests were gone."

So Gonzalez turned her attention to ecology, a passion that had always been in her family.

"My grandmother was an ecologist even though she died without ever hearing the word," she said. Gonzalez became an educator about nutrition and the environment. She worked with a group called the Comite de Agua (Water Committee). The group had four major victories during her time there—they prevented the building of a trash incinerator and a tire incinerator in the area, blocked the construction of an electrical generating station which would have damaged the environment, and halted the construction of two aquifers which would have pumped water away from poor communities to rich ones.

"We stopped the government from taking our water," she said. "The community worked all night taking the water out of the aquifers in 500 buckets and bringing it to the Congress. We told them, 'Don't take our water or we'll die of thirst.' It was a victory. I'm proud of being part of that. We fought for human rights and ecology."

Meanwhile Gonzalez was still in danger because of her

political work and was still suffering from the psychological effects of torture. In 1988, she relented to the requests of international friends and moved to Chicago, where she gained political asylum and received counseling at a center for torture survivors. She settled in Pilsen, a low-income mostly Mexican neighborhood on the southwest side of the city.

"Here I saw all the same problems as in my country," she said while cooking a pot of black beans, red and yellow lentils and rice in her spacious new home and office in Pilsen, obtained with the help of a local affordable housing group. "Kids in gangs, drugs, homeless people sleeping in the streets, domestic violence, alcoholism. It was just like I was in a barrio in my home country."

Wanting to do something to combat the local problems, she founded Ecovida, an urban ecology group. Ecovida started out with a small project at a local church, in which local kids raised tilapia fish in large bins, composted soil with worms in plastic tanks and grew organic vegetables in small indoor gardens with home-made recycled water systems. They sold the fish, vegetables and rich soil for a small income, in the process getting a taste of nature that is rare in the city, particularly in Pilsen, which is known to have the least green-space of any neighborhood in Chicago.

"Most of these kids are from campesino families, who worked the land in their home countries," she said. "They were uprooted from the earth and planted in concrete. Now it's like they're returning to the land."

Today Ecovida has grown into a major project, reaching over 1,000 students and adults per year. Along with running the local composting and organic gardening projects, Gonzalez teaches workshops in various Chicago elementary schools as well as at regional and national conferences. The walls of her home/ office are lined with photos of students in action, caring for plants and animals and learning about their links to the earth. One wall is blanketed with pictures the students have drawn to depict what they learned from Gonzalez. One colorful poster shows a menacing anthropomorphic purple blob of urban pollution reaching out to attack a cringing tree. The dining room is decorated with bundles of dry chili peppers and mangoes, also the result of Ecovida projects, and photos and plaques paying homage to slain Salvadoran bishop Oscar Romero and leftist Chilean leader Salvador Allende, who was toppled by a U.S.-sponsored coup in 1973. The refrigerator is decorated with construction paper and glitter art Gonzalez's grandson did at the nearby elementary school. She was reunited with her daughter Carolina, now 32, in Chicago after being separated from her during the war decades earlier. The two live with Gonzalez and help her with Ecovida.

The demands of Ecovida keep Gonzalez busy around the clock, but still the war and the struggle of her home country are never far from her mind.

In 2002, Gonzalez made international news when a Florida district court ruled in favor of her and two other plaintiffs who were suing two Salvadoran generals for torture and human rights violations. Under the Alien Tort Claims Act, which allows lawsuits in U.S. courts regarding matters that happened in foreign countries, the court ordered former National Guard director Eugenio Vides Casanova and former minister of defense Jose Guillermo Garcia to pay $54.6 million to Gonzalez and two other Salvadorans who were tortured during the war. The generals, now living in West Palm Beach, Florida, argued that they were not directly responsible for the atrocities carried out by their subordinates. But after months of painful testimony by the plaintiffs, the jury decided that the generals were responsible for the torture and human rights violations which were an intentional and systematic part of the war. While it remains to be seen if or when the payment will actually materialize, the verdict was seen as a victory for torture victims and survivors of civil war around the world.

With her easy laugh and warm, open smile, it is hard for

the people who know her now to imagine the horrors Gonzalez went through.

But she sees her current crusade—to bring healthy eating habits and respect and love for the earth to the children of immigrants and other urban dwellers in the U.S.—as part of the same struggle she waged in El Salvador.

"We're teaching our future generation to have a healthy world," she said. "Contamination by pesticides in the air, the water, the soil is violence against the earth. The contaminated food we eat is part of a food chain of violence. For me ecology isn't waving a political flag, but it is learning the politics of respect for human life and the environment. I'm trying to re-awaken people to this respect."

A detail of Marcos Raya's mural "Cataclysm" shows resistance in the immigrant neighborhood of Pilsen on the southwest side of Chicago. Art by Marcos Raya.

# Conclusion

It's obvious the clock can never be turned back on globalization and modernization in Latin America and other developing countries around the world, and most people wouldn't want it to be. Even as they fight to preserve their ancestral land and ways of life, many indigenous people and campesinos in Latin America also want access to the benefits of modernity—TV, cell phones, modern medicine. In an ideal world these innovations could be embraced along with traditional cultures and economies, with the two strengthening and complementing each other.

The internet has already proven a useful tool in organizing solidarity for grassroots resistance movements, from the Zapatistas in Chiapas to the CNTC campesino group in Honduras to the trade unionists in Colombia.

And while many in Latin America want to stay in their native communities and make a sustainable living, many would also love the opportunity to travel to or build a life in the U.S. or other countries for reasons other than out of economic necessity. Obviously citizens of the U.S. (or other "First World" countries) also have much to gain from contact with Latin American neighbors—different cultural values and knowledge; new political, intellectual and artistic ideas; a greater appreciation for the land; a larger understanding of the world in general. Ideally, the trade of goods and resources and the flow of people across borders need not be exploitative, but rather a logical form of global interaction.

So the question shouldn't be how can life for the Garifuna in Honduras or the Chol in Montes Azules be preserved as it has been for centuries, but rather how can "progress" proceed from here in a way that respects the human rights and dignity of all people, and isn't skewed to create massive wealth for a few on the backs of many. Furthermore who reaps the rewards of "progress," and how can "progress" be defined in a way that advances the health, quality of life and empowerment of people without destroying their very ways of life in the process?

Taking on the forces of global commerce and interconnected governmental power structures isn't an easy task. But old women in Bolivia or Ecuador wouldn't be taking to the streets to topple governments if there was no hope. Teenage boys wouldn't be hiking through blazing deserts along the U.S.-Mexico border to earn money for their families if there was no hope. Farmworkers from Haiti, Guatemala and Mexico wouldn't spend weeks riding a bus across the U.S. to camp outside Taco Bell's headquarters in California if there was no hope.

# Glossary of
# Terms and Acronyms

Campesino: A peasant farmer, someone who works a small plot of land for a subsistence level existence, or did until being displaced from that land. Many (but not all) campesinos are indigenous.

Chapare: Tropical region of Bolivia.

COCOCH: Consejo Coordinadora de Organizaciones Campesinos de Honduras, an umbrella organization of campesino groups in Honduras.

Coyotes: People who smuggle humans across borders, often for pricey fees.

CNTC: Central Nacional de Trabajadores del Campo, or National Center of Rural Workers, a militant campesino group in Honduras.

Colonias: The shantytowns in border cities like Tijuana and Reynosa where maquila workers typically live. Often they are essentially squatter communities, often without electricity or running water.

COMPA: Comunidad de Productores de Arte, the community arts organization in El Alto, Bolivia which works closely with the group Teatro Trono.

CONPAH: Confederación Nacional de Pueblos Autoctonos de Honduras, the National Confederation of Autonomous Indigenous People of Honduras.

Coordinadora: The Cochabamba, Bolivia-based Coordinadora Departmental por la Defensa del Agua (Committee for the Defense of Water), which led the "Water War."

EZLN: The Ejercito Zapatista por Liberación Nacional, or the Zapatistas, a rebel group in the state of Chiapas, Mexico demanding autonomy and dignity for indigenous people. The Zapatistas made their existence public with an armed takeover of the city San Cristobal de las Casas on Jan. 1, 1994, the day NAFTA took effect.

Free Trade: The reduction of tariffs, national subsidies and other measures that make it more profitable for multinational companies to do business in foreign nations, particularly developing countries where cheap labor is available. Often raw materials will come from one country, products will be assembled in another country and then the final goods will be sold in yet another country.

FTAA: The proposed Free Trade Area of the Americas, often called "NAFTA on steroids," would expand NAFTA-like provisions to 34 countries, basically all of Latin America except Cuba. ALCA in Spanish (Area Libre Comercial de las Americas).

Globalization: The catch-all phrase referring to the expansion of multinational companies and free trade agreements and the privatization of state industries, as well as the spread of culture and technology across borders. To critics, globalization is assumed to entail the exploitation of natural resources and the reduction of labor and environmental protections in the service of profit for multinational companies.

Indigenous: Native to a given land; in the case of this book a member of one of the 500-plus different peoples native to areas of Latin America, for example, the Quechua or Aymara in Bolivia, the Tseltal or Chol in southern Mexico or the Tulopane in Honduras. Under international conventions, many national constitutions and in keeping with their own beliefs, indigenous people are usually considered to have an intrinsic right to their ancestral lands.

INS: The Immigration and Naturalization Service, which formerly dealt with enforcement of immigration laws and legalization procedures. After the Sept. 11 terrorist attacks the INS was dissolved and its enforcement duties taken over by the Department of Homeland Security.

Lacandon: The extremely bio-diverse jungle area located in the state of Chiapas, Mexico; it is the site of conflicts between indigenous residents, the government and multinational companies with interest in logging, bio-prospecting or other pursuits.

Lacandones: Or the "so-called Lacandones," the indigenous group working in concert with the government in the Lacandon jungle. Their detractors point out that they originally migrated from the Yucatan peninsula.

La Migra: Spanish or Spanglish for immigration agents, former-ly the INS, though border enforcement is now carried out by the Department of Homeland Security.

Maquila, or maquiladora: The thousands of mostly foreign-owned factories that line the Mexican side of the border and are also located in cities within Mexico and other parts of Latin America. Maquilas take advantage of cheap labor forces to manufacture electronics, medical supplies, auto parts, clothing and countless other goods for export all over the world.

Mestizo: A person of mixed indigenous and other (usually white/ Spanish) heritage.

NAFTA: The North American Free Trade Agreement, institut-ed in 1994, largely obliterates tariffs and other protective measures between the U.S., Mexico and Canada. Numerous studies show Mexico has suffered negative economic consequences as a result of NAFTA.

Neoliberalism: The economic school of thought promoting free trade and globalization as the keys to prosperity and development.

OFRANEH: Organizacion Fraternal Negra de Honduras, the Black Fraternal Organization of Honduras, including the Garifuna and other African-descended people.

PPP: Plan Puebla-Panama, a large-scale manufacturing and transport project being carried out in Mexico and Central America, developed in part by the Inter-American Development Bank and pushed by Mexican president Vicente Fox. The plan includes a "dry canal" consisting of highways and rail lines from Panama up to the state of Puebla, Mexico, with industry including maquilas, industrial shrimp farms, eucalyptus plantations and hydroelectric dams lining the route.

Privatization: The selling off of formerly state-run industries like water, transportation, healthcare, gas or oil. Critics say privatization means profit is put ahead of services, and the population may lose guaranteed access to fundamental resources like water and healthcare. Proponents say private companies can run things more efficiently than government bureaucracies.

Pueblo: Roughly, "the people," as in a community or movement.

SINALTRAINAL: The Colombian trade union representing workers at Coca-Cola bottling plants around the country.

UCIZONI: A community group based on the Isthmus of Tehauntepec, in Oaxaca, Mexico. They are opposed to the PPP and free trade in general.

WTO: The World Trade Organization, a non-governmental legislative and judicial body which regulates trade and trade disputes and has the power to over-rule national laws and regulations particularly in regards to the environment. For example WTO panels composed of corporate attorneys have ruled that U.S. laws protecting sea turtles and dolphins and U.S. clean air standards are illegal barriers to free trade.

# Notes

1  Guillermoprieto, Alma. "The Heart That Bleeds: Latin America Now." First Vintage Books Edition, 1994. P. 249.

2  Americas Program, Interhemispheric Resource Center. "Seven Myths About NAFTA and Three Lessons for Latin America," November 2003.

3  Americas Program, Interhemispheric Resource Center. "Seven Myths About NAFTA and Three Lessons for Latin America," November 2003.

4  Pain, John. Associated Press, 10/29/03.

5  The Official Web Site of the Free Trade Area of the Americas (www.ftaa-alca.org).

6  Wallach, Lori. TomPaine.commonsense, "NAFTA on Steroids," 11/14/03.

7  Pain, John. Associated Press, 10/29/03.

8  Guillermoprieto, Alma. "The Heart That Bleeds: Latin America Now." First Vintage Books Edition, 1994. p. 187.

9  Shulman, Robin. *The Washington Post*, 11/2/03.

10  Davis, Mike. TomDispatch.com, "Bush and the Great Wall," 1/20/04.

11  "Root Cause People's March" organization, media reports.

12  The Service Employees International Union (SEIU) web site and materials, media reports.

13  The AFL-CIO web site, "Immigrant Workers Ride Triumphant," media reports.

14  Reuters, 8/7/02.

15  Barreda, Andres, La Jornada. 8/17/99.

16  Call, Wendy. " Information Access at the Inter-American Development Bank: The Case of the Plan Puebla-Panama." November 2003.

17  The Partido Revolucionario Institucional, which ruled Mexico for 71 years until President Vicente Fox's victory in 2000.

18  Call, Wendy. "Information Access at the Inter-American Development Bank: The Case of the Plan Puebla-Panama," November 2003.

19  Nelson, Jeremy. The Religious Task Force on Central America and Mexico's Central America/Mexico Report. "Mexico Peace Talks Falter as Indigenous Rights Bill Approved by Congress," Spring 2001.

20  Red Oaxaquena de Derechos Humanos, 2000.

21  Web report from Action for Social and Ecological Justice (ASEJ), Oct. 2003.

22  Indymedia Chiapas, 10/14/03.

23  The Puerto Rican island where the U.S. military conducted bombing exercises for years until a cease-fire in 2003.

24  Maderas del Pueblo del Sureste A.C. (Mexico). "No al desalojo!: El caso de la reserva Montes Azules en la selva lacandona…," June 2003.

25  Maderas del Pueblo del Sureste A.C. (Mexico). "No al desalojo!: El caso de la reserva Montes Azules en la selva lacandona...," June 2003.

26  Maderas del Pueblo del Sureste A.C. (Mexico). "No al desalojo!: El caso de la reserva Montes Azules en la selva lacandona...," June 2003.

27  Maderas del Pueblo del Sureste A.C. (Mexico). "No al desalojo!: El caso de la reserva Montes Azules en la selva lacandona...," June 2003.

28  Maderas del Pueblo del Sureste A.C. "Breve Historia de la Llamada Comunidad Lacandonia," December 2002.

29  Maderas del Pueblo del Sureste A.C. "Breve Historia de la Llamada Comunidad Lacandonia," December 2002.

30  Procaduria Federal de Proteccion al Ambiente.

31  Secretaria de Medio Ambiente, Recursos Naturales y Pesca.

32  International Labour Organization web site, "Indigenous Peoples."

33  Maderas del Pueblo del Sureste A.C. (Mexico). "No al desalojo!: El caso de la reserva Montes Azules en la selva lacandona...," June 2003.

34  Maderas del Pueblo del Sureste A.C. "Breve Historia de la Llamada Comunidad Lacandonia," December 2002.

35  Maariv Online, "Isuzu Challenge."

36  Press release "Rancho Esmeralda Invaded," 2/28/03.

37  Maderas del Pueblo del Sureste A.C. (Mexico). "No al desalojo!: El caso de la reserva Montes Azules en la selva lacandona...," June 2003.

38  Maderas del Pueblo del Sureste A.C. (Mexico). "No al desalojo!: El caso de la reserva Montes Azules en la selva lacandona...," June 2003.

39  CNN Interactive, 3/20/98.

40  Figueroa, Liliana. Cuarto Poder, 7/20/03.

41  The Arizona Republic, 6/19/03.

42  Ecuadorian National Institute of Statistics and Census, 2000.

43  Latin Focus, "Ecuador Unemployment 1990-2001."

44  Goodey, Jan. Red Pepper Online, "Guns, threats and exploitation behind the banana trade," December 2002.

45  Bussey, Jane. The Miami Herald, 3/10/00.

46  BBC News, 1/22/00.

47  Bussey, Jane. The Miami Herald, 3/10/00.

48  Hoag, Christina. Knight-Ridder Tribune, 10/29/03.

49  The Gray Rider Real Estate Company LLC, "An Overview of Honduran Real Estate Laws."

50  International Labour Organization web site, "List of Ratifications of International Labour Conventions."

51  National Confederation of Autonomous Indigenous People of Honduras (Confederación Nacional de Pueblos Autoctonos de Honduras).

52 Records kept by the CNTC (Central Nacional de Trabajadores del Campo.)

53 Lydersen, Kari. NACLA Report on the Americas, July/August 2002. (And local news reports and interviews.)

54 Consejo Coordinadora de Organizaciones Campesinos de Honduras

55 Central Nacional de Trabajadores del Campo.

56 Campaign to Stop Killer Coke. 2003.

57 Bacon, David. *The American Prospect.* 1/28/02.

58 U.S./Labor Education in the Americas Project (USLEAP), "Violence Against Colombian Trade Unionists Bulletin," 2003.

59 Campaign to Stop Killer Coke. 2003.

60 Campaign to Stop Killer Coke. 2003.

61 *Pittsburgh Business Times*, 7/20/01.

62 Panamco Annual Report 2002, "Colombia."

63 Network in Solidarity with the People of Guatemala report. 10/4/94.

64 Coca-Cola FEMSA web site, "Corporate Profile," 2003.

65 Van Yoder, Steven. Industry Week, 5/15/00.

66 International Union of Food, Agricultural, Hotel, Restaurant, Catering, Tobacco and Allied Workers' Associations.

67 International Union of Food, Agricultural, Hotel, Restaurant, Catering, Tobacco and Allied Workers' Associations. "Bulletin Number 3 - Coca Cola," 1998.

68 Vanautgaerden, Thomas. Web site "Coca-Cola," 1998.

69 Panamco web site as of 2000.

70 Panamco web site as of 2000.

71 Panamco 2002 Annual Report.

72 Alerta Laboral, monthly publication of the Centro de estudios para el desarollo laboral y agrario. Dec. 2003. p. 6.

73 Patzi, Felix. "Ya Es Otro Tiempo El Presente: Cuatro Momentos de Insurgencia Indigena." 2003. p. 261-268.

74 Patzi, Felix. "Ya Es Otro Tiempo El Presente: Cuatro Momentos de Insurgencia Indigena." 2003. p. 262.

75 PBS Frontline, "Bolivia: Leasing the Rain," June 2002.

76 Earthjustice.org.

77 Hacher, Sebastian. Corpwatch Web Site. "Argentina Water Privatization Scheme Runs Dry," 2/26/04.

78 PBS Frontline, "Bolivia: Leasing the Rain," June 2002.

79 Hacher, Sebastian. Corpwatch Web Site. "Argentina Water Privatization Scheme Runs Dry," 2/26/04.

80 Earthjustice.org.

81 PBS Frontline, "Bolivia: Leasing the Rain," June 2002.

82  "Tunupa," newsletter of Fundacion Solon. 7/2/03.

83  Yaku Al Sur, Bulletin #3. Published by the Coordinadora Departmental por la Defensa del Agua. Sept. 2003.

84  Patzi, Felix. "Ya Es Otro Tiempo El Presente: Cuatro Momentos de Insurgencia Indigena," 2003. p. 258.

85  Grimson, Alejandro and Edmundo Paz Solon, Programa de las Naciones Unidas para el Desarollo (PNUD). "Migrantes bolivianos en la Argentina y los Estados Unidos," 2000. p. 56-57.

86  Grimson, Alejandro and Edmundo Paz Solon, Programa de las Naciones Unidas para el Desarollo (PNUD). "Migrantes bolivianos en la Argentina y los Estados Unidos," 2000. p. 59.

87  Grimson, Alejandro and Edmundo Paz Solon, Programa de las Naciones Unidas para el Desarollo (PNUD). "Migrantes bolivianos en la Argentina y los Estados Unidos," 2000. p. 59.

88  Associated Press 2003, reprinted on NewsMax.com, 11/3/03.

89  Associated Press 2003, reprinted on NewsMax.com, 11/3/03.

90  Associated Press 2003, reprinted on NewsMax.com, 11/3/03.

91  Women on the Border, reprinted in "Puro Border," Cinco Puntos Press, 2003. p. 164.

92  Amnesty International. "Intolerable Killings: Ten years of Abductions and Murders in Ciudad Juárez and Chihuahua," Summer 2003.

93  U.S. Department of Health and Human Services, U.S.-Mexico Border Health Home Page, "Border Health Issues."

94  U.S. Department of Health and Human Services, U.S.-Mexico Border Health Home Page, "Demographics of the Border Region."

95  Dietz, Julia. Central America/Mexico Report by the Religious Task Force on Central America and Mexico, March 2003.

96  Sullivan, Kevin. *The Washington Post*, 2/16/03.

97  Sullivan, Kevin. *The Washington Post*, 2/16/03.

98  Procuraduria Federal de Proteccion al Ambiente.

99  Colectivo Chilpancingo Pro Justicia Ambiental (Tijuana) publication.

100 Environmental Health Coalition, "Plan de Saneamiento del sitio de metales y derivados en Tijuana, Baja California, Mexico," 5/16/03.

101 Newsletter of the Environmental Health Coalition, 5/16/03.

102 Environmental Health Coalition, "Plan de Saneamiento del sitio de metales y derivados en Tijuana, Baja California, Mexico," 5/16/03.

103 Cantlupe, Joe. *The San Diego Union Tribune*, 2/16/02.

104 Public Citizen, "NAFTA Chapter 11: Corporate Cases." 2003.

105 Chihuahua state documents obtained by Nuestras Hijas de Regreso a Casa.

106 Amnesty International, "Intolerable Killings: 10 Years of Abductions and Murders of Women in Cuidad Juarez and Chihuahua," August 2003.

107 Jordan, Sandra. *The Observer*, 11/2/03.

108 According to the local labor group CETLAC, Centro de Educativos y Taller Laboral A.C.

109 Portillo, Lourdes. "Señorita Extraviada." 2002.

110 Confederación de Trabajadores Mexicanos, or Mexican Workers Federation.

111 Delphi Electronics, www.delphi.com, 2003.

112 Robson, Ross."Shingo Prize News," shingoprize.org, 3/11/03.

113 Marizco, Mike. *Arizona Daily Star*, 9/9/03.

114 Moser, Bob. Southern Poverty Law Center Intelligence Report. "Open Season," Spring 2003.

115 Turf, Luke. *The Tucson Citizen*, 7/21/03.

116 Kamman, Jon. *The Arizona Republic*, 4/22/03.

117 Moser, Bob. Southern Poverty Law Center Intelligence Report. "Open Season," Spring 2003.

118 Moser, Bob. Southern Poverty Law Center Intelligence Report. "Open Season," Spring 2003.

119 Ibarra, Ignacio. *Arizona Daily Star*, 8/13/03.

120 Moser, Bob. Southern Poverty Law Center Intelligence Report. "Open Season," Spring 2003.

121 YumaSun.com, 5/9/03.

122 Gonzalez, Daniel. *The Arizona Republic*; reprinted in *The Tucson Citizen*, 4/30/03.

123 *Christian Science Monitor*, 7/14/03.

124 Carroll, Susan. *The Arizona Republic*, 7/30/03.

125 Marizco, Michael and Ignacio Ibarra. *The Arizona Daily Star*, 1/9/03.

126 Turf, Luke. *The Tucson Citizen*, 7/1/03.

127 Turf, Luke. *The Tucson Citizen*, 7/1/03.

128 Fernandez, Mireidy. *The Naples Daily News*, 3/16/02.

129 Legal filings for Mercedes Santiago Felipe in Hall County Court, Nebraska, 2001-2003.

130 Santana Jr., Norberto. *The San Diego Union Tribune*, 11/29/03.

131 Aduroja, Grace. *The Chicago Tribune*, 9/11/03.

132 Flaherty, Michael. *The Nation*, 9/12/02.

133 National Interfaith Committee on Worker Justice report, issued at the Labor Notes Conference in Dearborn, Mich. Sept. 2003.

134 National Employment Law Project, "Understanding the U.S. Supreme Court's Decision in Hoffman Plastic Compounds v. NLRB," April 2002.

135 Greenhouse, Steven. *The New York Times*, 10/25/03, 11/5/03.

136 Zook, Kristal Brent. Amnesty Now. "Hog Tied."

137 Zook, Kristal Brent. Amnesty Now. "Hog Tied."

138 Oppenheimer, Laura. *The Moline Dispatch*, 1/22/98.

139 *The San Jose Mercury News*, 11/29/03.

140 Sanchez, Leonel. *The San Diego Union Tribune*. 1/28/03.

141 Sanchez, Leonel. *The San Diego Union Tribune*. 1/28/03.

142 The Illinois Coalition for Immigrant and Refugee Rights and Heartland Alliance For Human Needs and Human Rights. "Immigrants of the Heartland: How Immigration is Revitalizing America's Midwest," June 2000.

143 Cainkar, Louise and Moushumi Beltangady. The Illinois Coalition for Immigrant and Refugee Rights. "The Changing Face of Illinois," October 2002.

144 Walker, Lynne. Copley News Service, 11/9/03.

145 ACLU San Diego, "U.N. Human Rights Panel Asked to Investigate Migrant Deaths on U.S. Border," 4/15/98.

146 Martinez, Roberto. Letter to San Diego Police Department Acting Chief John Welter, 6/10/03.

147 American Friends Service Committee, U.S.-Mexico Border Program. "Abuse Report 2001."

148 The National Training and Information Center (Chicago) and the National Coalition for the Homeless (Washington D.C.) web sites and reports.

149 Economic Policy Institute and Neighborhood Funders Group, "The National Study on Workers Centers," 5/28/03.

150 Worland, Gayle. *The Chicago Tribune*. 10/22/03.

151 Bowe, John. *The New Yorker*, 4/21/03.

152 Lydersen, Kari. *In These Times*, 2/16/04.

153 Bowe, John. *The New Yorker*, 4/21/03.

154 Bowe, John. *The New Yorker*, 4/21/03.

155 Lantigua, John. *The Palm Beach Post*, 12/21/03.

156 The Ford Foundation. "The New Nebraskans," Winter 2002.

157 Immigrant Rights Network of Iowa and Nebraska.

158 The Ford Foundation. "The New Nebraskans," Winter 2002.

159 Associated Press, 6/3/03.

160 Pierre, Robert. *The Washington Post*, 9/2/03.

# About the Author

Kari Lydersen reports for *The Washington Post* out of the midwest bureau and is an instructor with the Urban Youth International Journalism Program, working with youth who live in public housing or attend alternative high schools. She also writes about topics including immigration, prisons, labor issues and health care for publications including *The Chicago Reader*, *In*

Author photo by Victoria Cervante

*These Times*, *Punk Planet*, *LiP Magazine* and *Clamor Magazine*.

She is a former champion in open water swimming 15 and 25 kilometer events and a member of the swim team at Northwestern University, where she graduated in 1997. She grew up in San Diego and currently lives in Chicago.

Karilyde@yahoo.com.